Any Fool Can Be A Country Lover

JAMES ROBERTSON

Illustrated by Larry

PELHAM BOOKS

LONDON

First published in Great Britain by
Pelham Books Ltd
27 Wrights Lane
Kensington
London W8
1986

British Library Cataloguing Publication Data
Robertson, James, 1945–
Any fool can be a country lover.
1. Country life—England—West Country
2. West Country (England)—Social life
and customs
I. Title
942.3'0858'0924   S522.G7

ISBN 0 7207 1708 6

Typeset in 11 on 12½pt Baskerville Roman by
Cambrian Typesetters, Frimley, Surrey
Printed and bound in Great Britain by
Billing & Sons Limited, Worcester

Chapter One

THE GAMES of love have always been among the most popular pastimes of the human race. Down the centuries every possible aspect has been explored, discussed, observed, tried and perfected on countless occasions.

In the countryside, games started young. Even at the village primary school, the sexes were separate and different from their first day when little girls played house and little boys showed each other how to castrate piglets. By the age of eleven the advanced little boys were already torn between birds' egg collecting with their contemporaries and shy dalliance with the willing pre-liberated little girls. By their early teens the river bank was sighing and sobbing on the warm summer nights when the owls hooted and the fish plopped and unwary tender flesh all too often brushed against the darkened nettles.

When it rained, the world of the lovers closed in a little. The church porch was a favoured location; so too was the shelter on the common which housed the war memorial tablet. It was partitioned off into four sections sharing the same centre and each with one side open, so that four different couples could find out how far the girl was prepared to go and whether the boy was capable of taking her there. With the rain pattering down on the shingle roof to drown the cries and groans, the names on the tablet could look down at yet another generation of local youth, courting as did they themselves with no living witnesses save the bland-faced, incurious Charity Webber's sheep.

For adults, particularly married adults, it was more difficult. Middle-aged matrons were not as keen to besport themselves in the hayloft as they might once have been and the sophistication of a motel room was beyond both the pocket and the imagination of all but a tiny minority. But they made do. Snow brought out the gossips like truffle hounds: more than one couple had been found out as a result of incautious gumboot tracks leading to a remote barn from opposite directions. Caravans, many of which lurked in the corners of fields where they were part of the summer infrastructure geared to the goal of fleecing the tourists, took on their main role as popular winter trysting grounds.

This was the game of love. Occasionally, or even not so occasionally, the participants believed the game was real. Women, when they reached a certain age, often succumbed. They looked at their approaching middle years and their dull, farting husbands and rebelled. Some found careers; some found God; some found the books of Erica Jong and feminism; but many found themselves a lover. The onset of a grand passion could have catastrophic effects on the stability of the small society of the parish. Down the generations, virtually everyone had come to be related to everyone else and, if one marriage became mixed up with another, particularly if either should unscramble itself, the consequences could reverberate for years, reshuffling families and friends until all were ultimately forced to come to terms with added layers of complication on their kinship.

A certain expertise had developed among many of the local men in detecting those women who lifted their heads above the parapets of their marriage to sniff the air. It was Kelvin, a widower who had farmed in a Cro-Magnon way on the edge of the village for forty-five years, who first observed the onset of the symptoms in Mandy. It was very acute of him as most people had never noticed a tender feeling inside her and they would put any moodiness down to dyspepsia rather than to the yearning angst which preceded love. He told everyone about it in the pub.

'Mandy is a bit down in the mouth,' he announced after he had taken a long draught of beer and smacked the glass down on the counter. 'She was talking to the vicar after the service on Sunday.'

'Perhaps she was apologizing for not going to his services every week,' suggested Bill, another elderly farmer. He was rumoured to be bald but he never took his hat off so that one could see. He kept it on because that was where he kept his money. 'He must have had a nasty shock seeing you there.'

'I told him I only went because I wanted a look at that bloke who paid £180,000 for Redworthy Farm. He looked a right stupid idiot too. But Mandy was doing a lot of praying and she's not the sort to do much praying if she's in her right mind. Cursing – she'd do a lot of that, but not praying.'

'That's true,' reflected Bill. 'Now you mention it, I met her down by the river the other day reading a book. I asked her what it was and she gave me a real funny look and said that it was poetry.'

'Aha! You know what that means!' exclaimed Kelvin. 'Poetry! You know what women go and do when they start reading poetry! I thought it might be something like that when I saw her praying.'

There was silence round the bar as everyone considered the implications. 'Poor Keith!' remarked the commander, a man who had been on the receiving end of his own form of cuckoldry when his wife had decided to stop doing most of the work on their market garden and gone to Greenham Common.

'I should think Keith would be delighted,' replied Bill. 'It might give him a bit of peace if his wife concentrated on someone else.'

'That's quite true. But who the hell is there for her to concentrate on? There's the rub.' Malcolm Jarrett was an English teacher and was clever.

The drinkers uneasily let their mental files on the male population of the community riffle through in their heads. All the freely available males were too old, too drunk or too smelly. Moreover, Mandy had such a horrendous local reputation as a harridan that not even they would dare go near her. She was not bad-looking in a Thatcherite sort of way and would probably suit beautifully someone who had a

5

penchant for nannies in jackboots, but that was a sexual quirk that seemed to be unrepresented in the village.

'I'll have a chat to her when she's next in and see if I can pick up any information on what she's about,' volunteered Kelvin. The others looked at him with respect. Close encounters with Mandy were often dangerously unpleasant experiences as she had a general contempt for men, together with a tongue that could have polished diamonds. Granted, Kelvin would be in the enviable position of having original and authoritative gossip about her with which he could titillate the market by releasing it in dribs and drabs, but the price could be very high. The conversation moved on to the well-explored subject of the price paid by the idiot from upcountry for Redworthy.

Kelvin and Mandy coincided in the pub a couple of days later. The bar was as crowded as usual, with the regulars at one end. Mandy, who had been seen moodily pacing the common earlier in the day wearing a nylon fur coat and white gloves, ordered a cherry brandy and went to sit by herself in front of the fire which grizzled sullenly in the inglenook.

Kelvin topped up his pint as a precaution against being forced to buy Mandy one when his own ran out, received winks of encouragement from his peers and went over to fossick for information. Mandy looked up at him with eyes tragic with mascara. 'You're looking very nice this evening. Mandy,' he said with heavy gallantry. She was wearing sky-blue slacks and white high-heeled shoes.

'How very, very sweet of you to say so, Kelvin.' She managed to squeeze a tear and Kelvin watched with interest to see whether it would have the nerve to take the plunge and plough its way through her make-up. Its courage failed. 'Not many people seem to say nice things to me these days.' The tear was frozen by the onset of a speculative gleam generated in the eye behind it. Kelvin put as sympathetic a look as possible on his face. He was confident that his manifold drawbacks would soon kill the speculation. Even so, he thought it wise to waggle his grey false teeth warningly.

Mandy suppressed a tiny shudder and turned her gaze back to the fire.

'Tell me about it,' he breathed.

Normally such an encouragement from a source like Kelvin would silence even an insurance salesman, but Mandy was not in a normal frame of mind and she pulled a lace handkerchief from the sleeve of her cardigan to dab gently at her eyes. She then pulled out a compact, to inspect herself for damage. All was still secure. She looked round at Kelvin who had seized the moment to sit down beside her and light himself one of her king-size cigarettes. He gave an incredulous cough as the menthol hit the back of his throat and pitched the cigarette into the ashes of the fire.

'You're a kind, sensitive man,' said Mandy.

'I can't bear to see an unhappy woman,' replied Kelvin with simple insincerity. 'It'll help if you tell me about it.' The other drinkers were sitting silently by the bar, their ears twitching as they strove to hear the conversation by the fire.

Kelvin looked over, gave them a wink and moved even closer to Mandy. 'Is it Keith?' he whispered hoarsely.

'He doesn't understand me,' quavered Mandy.

'Is that right? How do you know?'

'He never talks to me when we're alone together, even when I tell him to.'

Kelvin clicked his tongue sympathetically. 'That must be terrible for you.'

'Yes. I need to know that I'm loved and I don't think Keith loves me any more.'

'I know Keith has a tremendous respect for you.'

'What the hell's the good of respect?' demanded Mandy with some force. 'I want to feel like a woman.'

'Perhaps Keith feels intimidated,' suggested Kelvin, knowing full well that Keith, like every other man in the village, had to suppress the urge to squeal with fright if Mandy so much as glanced at him.

Mandy looked thoughtful. 'Do you really think so? Intimidated. I didn't think of that. Do you think that Keith might really love me?'

The last thing that Kelvin wanted was that Mandy should start looking for fulfilment of her needs in her husband again. That would be extremely boring. 'You should know. How long is it that you've been married? Twenty years?'

'Twenty-two.'

'That's a long time. A very long time. A very, very long time. Any marriage must lose its sparkle after a quarter of a century.'

'How true!' murmured Mandy.

'You're an attractive woman, Mandy. It's a right shame if you're not appreciated.'

'You're really sweet, Kelvin,' murmured the unappreciated one. She placed an affectionate hand on his knobbly knee.

'If I was a younger man, Mandy . . .' Kelvin sighed a great theatrical sigh and drained his glass.

'Would you like another drink, Kelvin?'

'Oh, Mandy!' Unconsciously she had found the route to Kelvin's heart and, for a frightening few seconds, he teetered

8

on the edge of an emotional abyss before the imperative to fill his glass with free beer drove him to his feet and to the end of the bar away from the little group of regulars, ignoring their curious glances. He stood there, a shaken man, as Helga, whose mature Nordic beauty had launched a thousand extra barrels of beer in the year or two she had owned the pub, topped up his pint as he tapped his horny finger-nail nervously on the counter. Helga took her time about it. Kelvin liked a full pint, and if there was any trace of foam he would claim loudly that he was being cheated. Kelvin edged his way across to the others who opened to allow him into their midst.

'Have you thought of anyone?' he whispered hoarsely. Life had been going on while Kelvin had been by the fire and it took the others some time to catch up with what he was thinking.

Malcolm Jarrett got there first. 'Anyone for Mandy? It is like that, is it?'

'Yes,' whispered Kelvin.

'No,' said Malcolm.

'For Christ's sake. I need a name.'

'What's the hurry?'

'I'm beginning to fancy her. She's buying me this drink.'

To the credit of the others, Kelvin's urgency and the situation he was in did not drive them to mirth. There, but for the Grace of God, might go any of them. 'I don't see how having a name is going to help you out. But how about one of the men from the commune?' suggested Malcolm.

Kelvin's face cleared. 'Of course! That fellow Howard Something-or-other who quit the place last month! I haven't seen him with a girl for a fortnight. He'd be perfect.' He collected his drink and returned to Mandy. She smiled up as he approached. Kelvin sat down beside her and hummed a few bars of *Land of Hope and Glory* to show that he was at ease and that what was to follow was merely casual conversation. 'By the way, Mandy, I was talking to that fellow Howard—'

'Who's Howard?' Mandy demanded.

'You know. That man who left the commune the other day. He's moved in with that other ex-communard who goes

9

around in rabbit-skin waistcoats and does gardening. Dick – that's the other fellow.'

'No, I don't know him. What about him?'

'You must know him,' laboured Kelvin. 'He's that tall, handsome chap. The one with the light-coloured hair and the blue eyes. In his thirties. Anyway, he was asking me about you.'

'Asking about me?' Mandy incredulously put her hand on the shelf above her bosom. 'What did he want to know about me?'

'Just wanted to know who you were and a bit about you. He said that he would like to get to know you.'

'Did you tell him what I was like?' asked Mandy sharply.

Kelvin was very reassuring. 'Heavens, no! I said you were very nice. He's well-spoken too.'

'Mmm,' said Mandy thoughtfully. There was silence for half a minute or so. Kelvin stirred restively. He was unsure whether he needed to do any more selling. 'Blond hair, you said? And is he sensitive?'

Kelvin relaxed. 'Straight out of the commune. As sensitive as hairs on a stinging nettle.' Kelvin's metaphors could be bucolic but Mandy was oblivious. Her eyes were on the smoking fire, lost in a reverie that would have sold millions of copies if written between the covers of a Mills and Boon. Kelvin rose to his feet and tiptoed silently away.

The matter was only half-resolved. Mandy may have been pointed at Howard, but Howard needed to be pointed at Mandy before the men of the village could feel safe. There was not likely to be any trouble with Howard. He still had to redevelop his critical faculty after half a life spent immersed in blind faith in fashionable alternative philosophies. Any interest from Mandy would be grasped by him with the same delight he might show at a major pools win or a prettily shaped cloud.

Keith presented more of a problem. Kelvin and his cronies knew, through experience, that Mandy's delicate condition could lead to trouble, however they tried to avert it. All they could do was try to channel her in a direction in which she would do as little harm to anyone else as possible. But was it ethical not to consult Keith upon the subject? Some thought his heart would not grieve over what his eye did not see. Others that, as the husband, he had a right to know. There was also the problem of Napoleon, their teenage son. Did they owe any responsibility to him? Dennis, a middle-aged gentleman who also farmed, won the day.

'Napoleon? Why should we have to consider him? I saw him combing his hair in the post office the other day. Imagine it! Combing one's hair in public. I certainly don't think we need to worry about a youth like that! As far as Keith is concerned, I don't see any need to hide the good news. With a dragon like Mandy as a lifemate, he deserves to be told that he's due to have a break.'

'Right then, Dennis,' said Bill briskly. 'You can tell him the good news yourself and Kelvin can tell Howard.'

'I didn't mean that I should have to tell him,' objected Dennis. 'But I suppose somebody has to.'

All the various strands came together the following Saturday night. On Saturday nights the pub throbbed. There was dancing in a large room at the back to the sounds of Jason Loosemire and the Harvestmen with the emphasis on the Country rather than the Western. This brought in large droves of people from the surrounding towns and villages who, by 9pm, no longer minded that the music was appalling. There were other Saturday attractions. The skittle alley was usually the venue of a match against a rival pub which often brought along its darts team as well. Even the lounge bar had a traffic warden who came out to play olde tyme favourites on an organ. The only peace was to be found in the public bar where the barrier of scowling locals fixed strangers with beady, contemptuous eyes should they venture in from the fleshpots of pleasure in other parts of the establishment and usually managed to drive them out again. If a look failed, then Jimmy, the pub's most antiquated patron, would regurgitate a great gob of phlegm and hawk it ponderously and splashily on

11

to the toecap of his boot. Few stayed for long after that experience, and if they did they were probably the sort of company that the villagers liked to keep.

Mandy liked olde tyme organ music and so she and Keith were in the lounge bar, listening to the traffic warden. Howard gravitated to where the music was loudest and was to be found with his ear to the speaker through which Jason Loosemire's attempt at a Kentucky accent came whining, greatly amplified. The operation moved smoothly into action once it was discovered that all the protagonists were present and their various locations had been noted. First to peel himself from the bar was Dennis. He drained his pint and braced himself to move to the lounge and the sounds of *Danny Boy*.

Mandy was sitting near the organ with a faraway look in her eye. She had recently taken to using a long cigarette holder and Keith kept a good few feet from her in case of accidents, so Dennis had no trouble in hooking him away in order to talk. Keith was somewhat surprised to be hauled to his feet and dragged through the crush of olde tyme music lovers to a corner near the silent jukebox, but he did not query Dennis's right to do so. He had been conditioned by years of life with Mandy. Keith looked deeply down-trodden. He bared his teeth beneath his scrubby black moustache in a cringing grin.

'Hullo, Dennis.'

Dennis had not really thought about it before, but he had very limited experience in ways to tell a husband that his wife is probably going to have an affair and that it was something to rejoice about. He fumbled around for inspiration.

'Er . . . ah . . . hmph.' The fact that Keith was not a gentleman made it more difficult – not that Dennis had anything against him because of this, but it meant that they did not share the same language and attitudes. 'It's about the old girl. Would you mind frightfully if she . . . er . . . bolted?'

'Bolted? Old girl?' Keith was understandably puzzled.

'You know – Mandy.'

'What about her? She's over there.'

12

Dennis tried again. 'Er . . . have you noticed anything odd about her behaviour recently?'

Keith looked over at her. She was waving her holder dreamily to *Davy Crockett* coming from the increasingly flustered organist who was now competing with Jason Loosemire's imitation of Dolly Parton through the cob wall. 'No, I don't think so. She's looking for a lover, though. Do you mean that?'

'Er . . . yes, I suppose I do.' Dennis regarded Keith with astonishment. It was as if Mother Theresa had suddenly revealed a secret life as a mafia hit woman.

Keith continued without noticing Dennis's surprise. 'The problem is finding someone to take her on. It's been that way for years. It was dreadful in Reading. That's why we came here. There were all these parties and things and I got on all right, but Mandy was always left out. It was a real shame.'

'Heavens!' Dennis was having the same sort of feelings as must have been experienced by all those beautiful princesses of old immediately after they had kissed their frog. 'Are you saying that you and Mandy used to go to . . . er . . . *those* sort of parties?'

'Sure we did. But nobody would ever pick up my car keys. I had a Morris then and there was a big "M" on the key ring and everyone knew it was ours and so none of our friends – the men, that is – would ever pick it up. It was rather embarrassing to go home with someone else, knowing that Mandy was by herself.'

'You amaze me, Keith,' said Dennis faintly.

'No, really, it was difficult. Can you imagine leaving your wife behind in that situation? I used to feel so sorry for her. Anyway, eventually she couldn't stand it any longer and we moved down here. And it's just the same down here, really.'

'What?' exclaimed Dennis. 'You don't mean that there are parties like that round here?' Astonishment turned to injured vanity. 'I've never been asked to one.'

'No, I haven't found any parties. I wouldn't feel right about going to one anyway, after Reading. I'm just talking about . . . er . . . other friends.'

13

'Do you mean you've got a mistress?'

'Well . . . yes . . . I suppose you could call them that.'

'*Them?!*' echoed Dennis faintly.

The customers in the lounge broke into a spontaneous *King of the Wild Frontier* to accompany the climactic notes of the organ.

Dennis waited until the applause died down. 'You'd quite like it if Mandy found a "friend", then?'

'It would be wonderful', said Keith, turning and searching Dennis's face eagerly. 'It would get her off my back. Do you mean you fancy her?'

'Good God, no!'

Keith's face fell. 'Oh. Well, if you'll excuse me, he's playing *Sally* next. I must get back to her.' He scuttled through the crush back to his wife and Dennis slowly retraced his steps to the public bar.

It was an oasis of silence amid the jollifications taking place in the rest of the building. The problem of Mandy had given the patrons something different to concentrate upon and all were awaiting Dennis's report. A dozen pairs of eyes raked across his face as he entered. There was a dreadful possibility that Keith might have disapproved of the Plan and then they may have been forced to cancel it. Dennis did not look downhearted, nor did he look pleased. He just looked slightly stunned, which was uninformative. He went behind the bar to help himself to a large whisky. On Saturdays, the regulars were left to fend for themselves while Helga dispensed to the more profitable customers in other parts of the pub.

'Well?' demanded Malcolm. 'How did you get on?'

'Fine,' replied Dennis, sinking his scotch in one practised gulp before filling up once more. 'There'll be no problems with Keith. Quite the contrary. Kelvin might as well get on with it and have a word with Howard.'

'Not before you tell me exactly what happened. Did you actually tell Keith what was going on?'

'Not in so many words—'

'What the hell's the good of that?' shouted Kelvin. 'We

14

wanted to be quite sure what he felt about it. I mean he's the sort of bloke who'd string himself up in his barn if you so much as gave him a bollocking.' Kelvin paused. 'Except he hasn't got a barn, of course.' He paused again. 'He could always use someone else's, mark you.'

'I don't think there's much chance of that happening,' said Dennis.

'He's not stupid, you know. He's quite capable of working out that he could always use someone else's barn when he realizes he hasn't got one himself.'

'No. I mean he's not going to be too upset.'

'So you say. But if he should go and do something daft, I don't want it to be on my conscience.' Dennis could not help smiling, while a couple of others laughed outright. Kelvin looked puzzled. 'What did I say that was so funny?'

'I'm sorry,' Dennis apologized. 'It was just the idea of you having a conscience.' He walked round to the customer side of the bar. 'Honestly, there's no need to worry about Keith. He said they had to move down here because he was having lots of affairs and Mandy was jealous because she couldn't get fixed up.' There were incredulous looks from everyone. 'It's true. It really is. He also says that he's been . . . er . . . at it since he came down here – with more than one lady, too.'

'Don't be ridiculous!' scoffed Kelvin. 'He's been spinning you a yarn. Ladies, indeed!'

'It's difficult to believe, I know,' acknowledged Dennis. 'But I'm sure he was telling the truth. After all, it's so damn unlikely, he couldn't have made it up.'

There was a silence broken eventually by Malcolm. 'Women!' he said uneasily. 'I wonder who they might have been?'

'Or still are,' said Dennis, knocking back his second drink. 'Think on that!'

'It's astonishing,' said Bill. 'Who would have thought that Keith would be such a dark horse?' Bill was a bachelor and could afford to take a detached view of the affair or affairs.

'That's part of the trouble,' replied Malcolm, bring urban sophistication to bear. 'It's the ones you least suspect who do

15

it. A fellow like Frank Mattock who's all hairy chest and suntan are just talk and people like Keith are all action.' The question that was in everyone's mind was with whom he could be having his action.

The commander had been holding his peace until now. His Elfrieda was hardly the most desirable of women; on the other hand, nor was Keith the most desirable of men. The combination had the commander feverishly trying to work out whether he might be wearing a pair of horns. He dropped a 'hmm' into the silence. Everyone looked at him hopefully to discover whether he was about to contribute anything useful. 'I was wondering whether this might not change things a bit.'

'In what way?' asked Malcolm eagerly. He was feeling rather vulnerable since his was a modern, liberated relationship in which each partner respected each other's privacy and had their own friends. He trusted Stephanie, of course, and Keith was surely too much of a nonentity to be a threat, but there were no other wives who bounced round the lanes in running shorts and tee-shirt which displayed their charms to any passer-by.

'Well, I'm not sure that it would necessarily be a good idea to give Keith any more freedom. If what he says is true and if we get Mandy out of his hair, who knows what he might get up to next?'

'What do you mean?' asked Kelvin.

'If he can be as active as he appears to be with a wife who can make a lion whimper with a single glance, he might be round the parish like a bloody stoat if she gave him the nod. No woman would be safe. Not even your Prudence, Kelvin.'

'I bet my Prudence would be safe,' said Kelvin.

The commander was forced to agree. 'Well, no woman under eighty would be safe, except for Prudence.' The said lady, Kelvin's middle-aged daughter, did all the farming for her father. The last time she had been heard to utter in public had been a couple of months previously when she had thrown a 50-kilo bag of fertilizer at a hunt follower who failed to close a gate on the way through the farm. She had just missed him and broken her favourite dungfork. Then she had cursed.

16

Everyone considered the possibilities of Keith stoating round the village. The commander certainly had a point.

'I wonder how he does it?' mused Dennis. There was a faint note of yearning in his voice.

'Perhaps he understands women,' suggested Malcolm.

'I knew a fellow in the navy who said he understood women,' said the commander. 'Poor chap got his throat cut in a whorehouse in Marseilles.'

Kelvin brought the company back to the nub of the matter. 'If we do nothing about Mandy because you lot are scared of Keith, then she's going to be rampaging round the village looking for a fancy man – and if that happens, God help us all. I know what I'm going to do and that's go and tell Howard that Mandy fancies him.' He heaved himself off his barstool, deftly lifted Bill's almost untouched pint without its owner noticing and moved hurriedly towards the door. Nobody made a move to stop him, not even Malcolm.

Mandy was determined to wring every possible ounce of romance out of her experience. As the prime consumer of bodice-ripping fiction from the mobile library, she had very clear ideas about how things ought to progress. They should not be hurried. The First Encounter was on Monday morning. Howard had come in on his bicycle to cash a Social Security cheque. Mandy, who must have peeking through her curtains, saw him cross the bridge into the village and she hurried up to the post office after him, bearing a letter. It was as well for the community information network that Maud, who ran the establishment, was an imaginative and dedicated gossip – as a cousin three times over to Kelvin, it was in her genes.

Howard had collected his money and was engrossed in a pamphlet about the importance of opening a National Savings account by the time that the panting Mandy crashed through the door. She strutted up to the counter to buy her stamp, waggling her hips at him. Howard did not appear to notice. All was grist to Howard's undiscriminating mental mill and his concentration on the prognosis for £5 a month over five years was total. Mandy turned and dropped her letter at his

17

feet. It was not enough so, her lips tightened, she kicked him sharply on the ankle. The average man would have looked at Mandy to see why he was being kicked, but Howard looked down at his ankle to see what had disturbed it. His butterfly mind was easily distracted by the letter, lying by his foot.

'Hey! Somebody's dropped a letter.' He looked up at Mandy. He recognized her, which was quite an achievement. 'You're Mandy, right?'

Mandy fluttered her eyelashes. Her best feature was her vivid blue eyes which she framed in sets of stick-on lashes that could have been used to whitewash a ceiling. As they flapped, they stirred tiny clouds of powder and mascara which swirled and eddied round her cheeks. 'La, sir,' she said.

Howard was not a reader of romantic fiction and failed to recognize a Cartland come-on when he heard it. 'You'd better pick up your letter.'

Mandy looked at him critically. It was obviously his job to pick up the letter. No romantic hero would expect her to do it. But she had to make allowances for ignorance and the fact that he had spent many years being brainwashed by a

succession of gurus in a succession of communes. If Howard would follow a louse-infested, half-naked Indian fakir, it certainly was not beyond her capabilities to make him follow her and he looked as if he would be worth the effort – tall and slim with a delicious little bottom. The clincher was that he was interested in her. 'You pick up the letter,' she ordered.

This course of action had not occurred to Howard, but he greeted it with his customary enthusiasm. 'Hey! Yes. That's a good idea. I never thought of that!' He smiled happily.

'Well, do it then,' said Mandy patiently. She was beginning to learn.

'Gosh, yes. I'll pick it up.' He bent down, took the letter and studied it. It was addressed to Littlewoods. With a remarkable demonstration of initiative, he noted the fact that it was stamped, turned it over and checked that it was sealed before slipping it through the slot into the postbox. He turned proudly back to Mandy. 'There!'

Maud, who was watching with open interest, nearly burst into applause. Her choked cheer earned her an icy look before Mandy, her eyelashes clapping like the wings of a pheasant at take-off, flashed him a beaming smile of thanks. She had had an excellent dentist and so her smile was quite impressive. 'You are so very, very kind.'

'Hey! That's nice: "You're very kind." Oh yeah.' Howard had a short memory span. 'You're Mandy, aren't you? Kelvin was telling me about you. I think that's really nice. I really like your eyelashes. They're really thick.'

'Oh, thank you very much,' Mandy managed to summon a blush almost as deep as Hermione Grimshaw's in *Master of Darrowby*. It was not too difficult as this was more the sort of thing she was after.

'Where did you buy them?'

Chapter Two

IT IS WELL known that the course of true love never did run smooth. The evening after Mandy and Howard had commenced their liaison, the pub was disturbed when Howard came in with an alternative girl on his arm. A communard, or even an ex-communard like Howard, could be put in the middle of the Sahara Desert for half an hour and he would emerge with a short girl with no conversation and large breasts, clothed from head to toe in cast-offs from an Oxfam shop. Nobody quite knew where these females came from. There had been a festival at the commune a few years back where stalls sold candles, jewellery made from horseshoe nails, and various kinds of food that equated lack of hygiene with wholeness, while guitarists and troubadours dirged away or turned laboured cartwheels to amuse the public. Then the lanes round the village were filled with these young women. They could be found on roadside verges sitting in crosslegged meditation with a corona of dun-coloured clothing round them or in tight and intimate embrace with their scrawny, bearded male counterparts.

The girl with Howard was typical of the breed: a bush of straight brown hair through which a nose could be seen and a great shapeless bundle of clothing that covered any contours she might have had. Howard led her to one of the rough oak tables that were against the wall and sat her down before coming towards the bar to order drinks. With the eyes of the pub on her, she pulled out a tobacco tin, expertly rolled herself a cigarette which she lit, and then stared at the wall in front of her. The pub followed her gaze, but there was only a rather mean set of antlers on the wall with a plaque which told that the stag that had worn them had been accounted for at Horney Bottom in 1925. The pub then turned back to Howard as he waited by the bar. It frowned at him and he bared his teeth in a smile.

'What do you think you're up to?' demanded Kelvin.

Howard had had a hard day. Lots of attention and lots of things being expected of him. 'What do you mean?'

'Well, you were going out with Mandy yesterday and you've got a different woman now. You can't do that sort of thing round here. It's not like it is upcountry, you know.'

Howard wrinkled his brow. 'Mandy was my karma yesterday. She might well be it tomorrow. But today's today.'

Once Kelvin had worked out his meaning, he drew in his breath sharply. 'That's immoral.'

'Yeah,' replied Howard happily. 'Isn't it great?'

Kelvin did not know what the world was coming to and so he shook his head sadly and turned deliberately back to his pint.

Malcolm then tried to make Howard understand the implications of his actions. 'Did you know Mandy was due in this evening?' he asked innocently.

Howard turned to him, his face lighting up. 'Is she? Good. I'm sure she'd like to meet Sweetbriar.'

Malcolm did not even flinch. 'I wouldn't be so sure about that,' he said drily.

'Don't waste your breath,' remarked Kelvin. 'That bugger won't have the faintest idea of what you're talking about.' Kelvin knew his man. Howard had forgotten about the concepts like jealousy which make us human. He looked puzzled, shrugged and took his drinks back to Sweetbriar.

'What time do you think Mandy and Keith will be in?' asked the commander.

Kelvin looked up at the old station clock that hung on the wall above the bar. He did not wear a watch. 'It's Tuesday, so they'll be here in ten minutes.'

'Oh dear,' moaned the commander. 'I'm not sure that I'm looking forward to that.' An outsider might have considered that an over-reaction, but there were no outsiders present and all knew Mandy. However, the cohesion of the mob gave everyone the moral strength to wait until the pub door opened to allow Mandy's and Keith's entry.

Mandy was first, her loose sheepskin jacket filling the doorway. She swept in, her handbag dangling over her arm, and looked slowly round the room as she waited for Keith to escort her to the bar. Her eyes reached the eyrie that was Sweetbriar's hair and saw Howard's head behind it. Theirs were the only two heads in the pub that had not automatically swivelled to see who was coming in. Mandy turned pale. Her hand flew to her throat, the handbag on her arm clouting the back of the head of Mr Loosemire, the local postman and peeping tom, who was enjoying a quiet drink with his wife. His cry of pain – Mandy's bag was loaded with bottles of scent and heavy-duty deodorant – penetrated through the concentrated attention between Howard and Sweetbriar and they looked over. Howard recognized, smiled and pulled Sweetbriar to her feet to bring her over.

'Hey there, Mandy!'

'Judas!' Mandy hissed. 'Are you so faithless that you cannot remain true for a day?'

'What's that?' demanded the puzzled Howard. He shrugged uncomprehendingly. 'Anyway, I thought you might like to meet a friend of mine. This is Sweetbriar. I have been telling her about you.'

'Keith!'

Keith had been engaged in hanging up his coat on the line of pegs beside the door. Years of conditioning made him drop his coat to the floor at the first consonant of the call and, by the time that her mouth was closing behind the last spat lisp, he was by her side. 'Yes, dear?'

'This . . . this libertine has insulted me. Do something about it.'

Howard and Keith looked at each other in dismay. The first did not know what he had done wrong and the second did not know what he was supposed to do about it. 'Er . . .' faltered Keith.

Mandy had been enjoying being the heroine of a romantic novel all day. She had been through the Encounter and the Dawning Realization. The Quarrel was not due until after the Declaration, while Betrayal was a chapter she had never liked anyway. She brushed Keith aside and brought down her stiletto heel hard on Howard's toe. Poor Howard was wearing trainers as usual, but he had a defender to hand.

From beneath the eyrie emerged an eagle. 'You bloody old cow!' yelled Sweetbriar. 'You did that deliberately!' She was carrying a glass of lager which she emptied down Mandy's front.

Violence was very rare in the pub, so there was consternation round the room as Mandy, breathing heavily, removed her soggy coat and handed it to Keith before advancing on Sweetbriar. Howard and Keith clutched each other in alarm while there was a scrape of barstools as the regulars drew back for fear of flying beer or glasses.

23

It was the commander's luck to have chosen to visit the lavatory shortly before Mandy and Keith arrived. His route back to the bar led directly between the two protagonists. Since he was there already and nobody else showed much inclination to become involved, he thought he might try to maintain the peace. With his back to Mandy, he waved his arms, shooing Sweetbriar back towards her table. He met with little resistance. She was beginning to realize that she was in danger of being consumed by a primeval force rather more tangible than ley lines or planetary influences. 'Get her out of here!' shouted the commander over his shoulder at Keith. Keith chose to misunderstand. He abandoned Howard, side-stepped neatly round the commander and put his arm round Sweetbriar. The cool efficiency with which his hand casually thrust its way into her clothing to establish that there really was a breast in there somewhere was quickly noted by the pub as the first tangible evidence that he might be the lounge lizard Dennis claimed him to be, but Mandy was still the prime focus of attention. The commander turned fearfully back towards her, his shoulders hunched ready to ward off any blow. He was right to be worried. Mandy was standing looking at him with her lips slightly ajar, a dazed look in her eyes. 'Commander! You were wonderful! You saved me!'

'What?'

'You came to my rescue when I might have been hurt. Commander! Oh, Commander!' Mandy gazed at him, her eyes shining.

There was a hiss of indrawn breath from the barstools and the commander suddenly understood. 'Oh God! No! I didn't, really I didn't. It was Keith. Look, over there! See? Keith is still protecting you. Aren't you, Keith?' But Keith was concentrating on charming Sweetbriar. The commander turned desperately to Kelvin for confirmation. 'He is, isn't he, Kelvin?'

Kelvin considered. His love of seeing someone else in trouble warred with his feeling that some troubles should not be wished on a dog. Regretfully he spoke. 'That's right, Mandy. It's Keith who's protecting you all right.'

'That's true,' agreed Bill, a man more generous of spirit, and Malcolm grunted concurrence as well.

But they might well have saved their breath. Mandy's plot had changed. A Gallant Knight had come to her rescue. The commander was doomed.

Mandy smiled with the smile that Andromeda must have used when she saw Perseus wearing his winged sandals, flapping across the sea towards the rock to which she was chained. 'You were wonderful, Commander. It's just like you to be so modest. Elfrieda is a lucky girl to have you as her husband. She's away this week, isn't she?'

'Shit!' said the commander, as he tore himself from Mandy's adoring gaze and staggered out through the door of the pub and into the night, his eyes bleak with the fearful knowledge of the future.

Mandy called after him, 'Good night. I'll pop in to thank you tomorrow morning!'

Chapter Three

MANDY'S INFATUATION with the commander was to prove the first harbinger of a disturbed autumn and winter. The second was Ivor's decision to hold a village day. He was chairman of the parish council, a man of considerable power whose chief interest lay in commentating through loudspeakers at events like gymkhanas and point-to-points. Unfortunately the tide of progress had caught up with him and his chosen field was now cluttered by smooth-talking youths with the glamorous crowd-attracting qualification of playing records on the local radio station. If he could not persuade the organizers of such events to come to him, he would create his own and was open to ideas.

Somebody suggested an exhibition of village history. Somebody else suggested dancing on the common, even though it would be October. Ideas snowballed, only to melt away when it was realized that someone would have to take responsibility for translating them into practice. However, the village day had the wholehearted support of the entire community so long as nobody was expected to provide any practical assistance in making it happen. Everyone congratulated everyone else on such an exciting idea and then forgot about it, secure in the knowledge that it would come to nothing.

Three people ensured that the carnival did not die: Ivor, who wanted to loudspeak; Lindy, the district nurse; and Dick. The last named, like Howard, was a graduate from the commune, although he had had a couple of years away from it to clear the cobwebs from his brain. He earned a precarious living as a professional countryman from an old farmhouse into which he had recently moved. He rented it from the owner, last twig on the tree of a family that had farmed there since 1620, who now ran a kosher delicatessen in Toronto. He caught and ate rabbits and deer, feasted on blackberries, mushrooms and nettles and sold things made from fur and bits of wood to tourists. He dressed like Bilbo Baggins in a brown tweed suit and moleskin waistcoat, made from real moles, which disturbed the squire since the suit, once his favourite, had been given by his wife to a jumble sale without his knowledge.

Dick did not often come into the pub because he never had much ready cash and because he both brewed and grew his own intoxicants. When he did come in, he remained in character, so tended to sit by the fire nursing a glass of beer and saying very little but looking wise. It impressed visitors but the effect was always spoiled if he spoke when Black instead of West Country issued from his mouth. On this occasion he came right to the bar and spoke. 'Who's organizing the historical exhibition?'

'What historical exhibition?' inquired Mandy. She was waiting for the commander, but the commander did not now come to the pub in the evenings unless he could see the television flickering behind Mandy's lace curtains.

'The one that's going to be part of the village day.'

'Oh that! Why do you want to know?'

'Because I've got something that ought to go in.'

'What?' asked Malcolm.

'A turtle. I found it in my garden.'

'Ah, yes! Of course.' Malcolm was reluctant to follow the conversation further for fear of it entering the uncharted waters of communard lunacy, so he carefully lit a cigarette, leaving it to someone else to pick up the baton.

Kelvin obliged. 'What has the history of the village got to do with a turtle? And what the hell's it doing in your garden? I haven't heard of many of them round here.'

'That's true,' agreed Bill. 'I've only seen them in the sea. On television, that is. I suppose you might have them coming up the river.' He turned to Keith whose cottage virtually fronted on the river. 'Have you seen many turtles about?'

'I can't say that I have. But it could easily be a tortoise. They look like turtles and it could be an escaped pet.'

Dick laughed. 'It's a fossil turtle, not a live one.'

Kelvin turned to Bill. 'Fossil?' he asked under his breath.

'Turned to stone. Like those dinosaur bones.'

'I thought it might make an interesting exhibit to show that strange creatures used to live in the area,' continued Dick.

'They still do,' said Kelvin caustically.

'Where did you come across this fossil turtle?' asked Malcolm.

'It was rather odd. I was planting comfrey and found it just below the surface of the soil. It's more than two feet long and very heavy. You can see the markings on the shell quite clearly.'

'Why were you planting comfrey?' asked Kelvin.

'Comfrey? It's a vulnery.'

Kelvin looked at Malcolm, but he shrugged. 'What's a vulnery?'

'You put it on wounds.'

'Oh,' said Kelvin. 'Why don't you use sticking plaster?'

'Comfrey heals bones as well.'

'Splints,' contributed Kelvin wisely. 'Splints is the best thing for broken bones. When I broke my arm – it must be twenty years ago now – I had to put on a splint for a couple of months. Nobody mentioned anything about comfrey. It's not a proper medecine anyway. It's a plant.'

'That's what antibiotics were, plants,' said Malcolm.

'Don't be stupid. They're pills. You don't see pill plants growing in the hedges.'

'But penicillin is the mould on top of jam. Fleming first discovered it growing on a culture dish in Paddington Hospital.'

Kelvin's scorn was unassailable. 'It was probably soot from the Cornish Express. That went into Paddington. Pills are white anyway and mould is black.'

'About my turtle fossil—' interrupted Dick.

28

'I don't believe it can be a turtle fossil,' said Ivor. 'You just don't get fossils lying about in flower beds. They are in quarries and coal mines.'

'True,' agreed Dick. 'But some previous inhabitant of the farm might have found it somewhere and brought it back home.'

'Your house was lived in by Percy Bladderwort and his father and grandfather before him. Those Bladderworts were so thick they wouldn't bring home a nugget of gold, let alone a dirty great stone tortoise.'

'Why don't we go down and look at it?' suggested Malcolm. 'I would quite like to see it.'

'Why don't you?' invited Dick.

'If you go down that lane of yours in anything less than a four-wheel drive, you could be there forever,' said Kelvin scathingly.

'What have you been doing coming down my lane?' asked Dick.

'I wooed Chastity Bladderwort forty years ago and that lane was pretty bad then, and it was no better when I went to Percy Bladderwort's wake. That old fool owed me a fiver for a bag of potatoes when he died. I've got better things to do than look at dead tortoises.'

'Well, I'd like to see it,' said Malcolm. 'Can I buy you a drink?'

'Thank you. I'll have a glass of water.'

It was probably the first time that such a sentence had been uttered within those walls since John Wesley may or may not have had lunch there in 1759 or 1765. Certainly the stunned silence in the room was broken by a sudden gust of wind down the chimney which could only have been the ghosts of generations of villagers who had cheerfully puked cider out on the verges of the lanes on the way home of a night.

Kelvin shuddered. 'Why?'

'I've got Sweetbriar staying with me and she recommended tincture of campion for my feet and I can't have any alcohol for an hour after taking it.'

'What's wrong with your feet?'

29

'An ingrowing toenail.'

'And you'd turn down a free drink because of an ingrowing toenail? You stupid Jessie!'

In the end, Lindy was appointed to organize the historical exhibition. As district nurse, she toured the countryside all day visiting the sick, the lame, the old and the slightly mad – just about everyone, in fact. So it was reckoned that she knew where possible exhibits might lie. Her first duty was to go down to inspect the turtle. Mandy came along too so that she could inspect Sweetbriar. Mandy would have gone by herself but she preferred to risk Lindy's car down the lane to the cottage rather than her own. She was giving a home for a fortnight to a Yorkshire terrier belonging to her hairdresser who had gone to Corfu for a late holiday and suspected that the animal might be car-sick – another reason for preferring Lindy's car.

The lane was everything Kelvin had promised. Centuries of rain and generations of cattle had worn it well below the level of the adjoining fields and the ash, oak and beech on each hedgebank had joined to create a tunnel whose floor was littered with water-filled potholes that were home to whirligig beetles, water boatmen and the occasional stickleback. It took ten minutes to drive the few hundred yards to Dick's house and once Mandy found herself unceremoniously ejected from the car to sound a pothole on the surface of which Lindy thought she saw the spreading rings left by a trout rise.

Their route crept round the side of a crumbling stone barn and they drew up on a small open space ringed by unkempt trees and bushes. On one side was the house, its windows almost invisible under a thick coat of ivy. Lindy looked at it uneasily. 'It must be dying for a good scratch.'

'It looks damned unhygienic,' sniffed Mandy. 'Probably full of rats.'

Mandy attached a thin chain leash to the dog's collar and they walked to the door. The ivy lapped at its edges as Lindy hammered on the knocker. The oak plank door creaked open on rusty strap hinges to reveal a large dank hall, its wooden walls covered in flaking grey paint. The two women looked at

30

each other nervously, but the terrier trotted ahead and lifted its leg against a line of scuffed and muddy gumboots by the wall. Mandy tugged on the chain and it hopped back, spraying the stone-flagged floor. She looked at it with distaste. 'Dirty little brute.'

'Come in!' shouted a voice from the interior of the house. 'I'll be with you in a second. I'm just skinning a hare.'

They stepped inside, looking at the half-dozen doors that led off the hall and wondering which concealed Dick or Sweetbriar. The hall was dominated by an immense print of one of Landseer's more Rambo-like stags. Trapped behind the glass were the desiccated corpses of several tortoiseshell butterflies. On another wall there was Dick's famous collection of antlers. In his initial revolt against the ethics of the commune, he had gone through a Daniel Boone phase, but he was in the process of reverting to organic environmentalism. Among the antlers was an Ordnance Survey map of the district crisscrossed by black felt-tip pen lines. 'What are those lines?' asked Mandy coming over to join Lindy.

'They're ley lines, I think,' replied the nurse.

'I knew it. He's really just a communard!'

The door behind them suddenly opened to show Howard framed in the doorway, wearing his jeans but displaying his sinewy torso. He was, of course, delighted to see them.

'Hey, great to see you, Mandy. Hey, it's really nice.'

Mandy's nostrils flared. She had switched to the commander but she had not told Howard. He was supposed to be still pining for the love of her and was due to have his heart broken when Mandy got round to telling him that she loved another. 'Howard! What are you doing here?'

'Staying with Sweetbriar—' A look of concern crossed his face. 'Are you feeling all right?'

Mandy had leaned back against the wall and put her hand to her breast, a look of pain on her face.

Howard went over to her and grasped her hand. 'Is it heartburn? Very painful, heartburn.'

Mandy snatched her hand away. 'How could you? You . . . you rake!'

31

Howard backed bewilderedly into the room from which he had emerged. 'Hey, that's a bit heavy. What's the matter?'

Mandy, breathing heavily, followed him through the door.

'Faithless bastard!' she hissed.

'Wuff!' agreed the dog, having no choice but to follow since the lead was round her wrist.

It was a bedroom, the floor littered with discarded clothes and the air blue with the smoke from a cluster of joss-sticks that were stuck in a vase on a pine chest of drawers. Sweetbriar was crosslegged on the bed examining a plastic daffodil on the blanket in front of her.

'Oh!' cried Mandy in horror, her hand flying to her throat. The dog, which had been sniffing the atmosphere in disgust, let out a gurgle as its collar tightened against its throat. 'You betrayed me, you seducer!'

Howard appealed to Lindy who was cautiously looking round the edge of the door. 'Lindy! Help me!'

'That's right! Bring another woman into it! Aren't two enough for you? If that ridiculous child can be called a woman!' Mandy had been expecting Sweetbriar to react with guilt and shame but, when she did not react at all, she went over to look at her. 'What's wrong with her?' she asked as Sweetbriar continued her scrutiny of the daffodil.

'She's meditating,' replied Howard.

Mandy stepped back from the bed. 'No!' she cried. 'You've drugged her! You degenerate!'

Lindy was standing in the doorway. 'For heaven's sake, Mandy. Stop being so overdramatic.'

Mandy stepped back another pace and struck a pose. There was a shriek of anguish from Howard. 'My jacket! You're standing on my buckskin jacket!'

'Sod your jacket!' replied Mandy, grinding it into the floor with the stiletto heel of her red boot. Howard bent down and tugged sharply at his jacket. There was a crack as Mandy's heel broke off the boot. The room froze; even Sweetbriar cocked a wary eye away from her daffodil.

'You bastard! Look what you've gone and done!'

32

Mandy had always been verbally violent but the power of love made her translate words into action for the second time within a few days. Howard retreated towards the window, managing to avoid a wild haymaker from her left hand. She limped towards him and delivered the follow-through. This came from her right hand which was attached to the dog's leash.

The animal was lifted off its feet, hurtled through the air just above Howard's head and crashed through the window, taking with it two panes and the wooden batten that supported them.

'Shit!' said Mandy, momentarily distracted from Howard. The latter seized the opportunity to grab his shirt and scuttle round her out of the bedroom. There was the sound of the front door of the house opening and he could be seen running up the lane, tucking his shirt into his trousers. His progress was slow as he had been forced to leave his shoes and socks behind. Mandy, Lindy and Sweetbriar went over to the window to watch him go. 'Swine!' exclaimed Mandy with considerable venom, peering through the ivy at his disappearing figure.

'What *is* going on here?' said Dick from behind them.

'There's been a bit of a disagreement between Mandy and Howard,' explained Lindy.

'Why is my window broken?'

'Mandy swung her dog through it,' contributed Sweetbriar. 'It made quite a crash.'

'I know. I heard it. And where is it?'

'Where's what?' asked Lindy.

'The dog.'

One end of the leash was still wound round Mandy's wrist. Everyone looked at it and followed the chain which disappeared out of the window. 'Damn!' said Mandy, hauling in her line. The head of the dog appeared above the window sill.

'Oh! Poor little thing. Be careful!' said Sweetbriar as it rolled its eyes at those inside the room. They were bulging slightly which was not surprising as it was hanging from its collar several feet above the ground. Sweetbriar rushed forward and picked it up, cradling it in her arms. 'It's bleeding!' she exclaimed.

'I'm not surprised,' said Lindy. 'You'd be likely to be cut about a bit if you had been flung through a window. Let me have a look at it.'

The dog had realized that it was safe within the protection of Sweetbriar's bosom and had relaxed enough to begin shivering as Lindy touched it. 'Where's it bleeding?'

'I felt blood on my front,' replied Sweetbriar.

Lindy ruffled through the dog's fur and then looked at Sweetbriar's shirt. 'It's all right. I don't think it's been cut.' The dog was looking as pathetic as only a Yorkshire terrier can. 'Mandy, that was really a dreadful thing to do.'

'I was provoked,' replied Mandy sullenly. 'The dog's OK. Aren't you, Flossie?'

Flossie was quite happy where she was and cowered deeper into her valley of safety. Sweetbriar peered down through her hair. 'Are you sure the poor little thing's all right? I could have sworn I felt blood.'

'It was probably urine,' said Lindy briefly. 'It's peed down your shirt.'

Sweetbriar opened her arms. The dog did not fall straight down as Mandy had some tension on its collar from the leash. It fell in an arc against Mandy's leg and promptly sank its teeth into her ankle. A defensive compensation for being tiny was that it had teeth like hypodermic needles. Mandy grunted and kicked out, dislodging Flossie and sending her across the floor towards Dick. The dog's collar snapped this time as Dick neatly sidestepped to allow the animal to slide through the door.

'*You'd* probably piss yourself if you had been defenestrated,' he observed.

Flossie was not finished. She picked herself off the floor – she had not got far to go – shook herself and then darted through to nip Mandy's other ankle. The little animal dodged her kick, skipped round Dick, shot through the front door and took off up the lane after Howard.

'What are you doing here, anyway?' asked Dick as they all

34

watched the dog through the window. 'Apart from breaking up my house and driving away my guests.' He turned to Sweetbriar. 'What was that about, by the way?'

'That was Howard. He was a friend of mine,' said Mandy. 'He made me extremely cross.'

'Yes, I can see that,' replied Dick drily. 'Your eyes flash and you flare your nostrils like a dragon.'

Mandy looked at him suspiciously. 'Are you calling me a dragon?'

Dick hastily raised his arms in protest. He had realized that it was unwise to provoke her. 'Certainly not. You don't look the least like a dragon. You're most attractive. Perhaps a bit of a fire breather.'

'Attractive?' repeated Mandy. She gazed at Dick with a musing look on her face. Lindy feared for him but Mandy had just had a lesson in emotional pain and was not yet ready to switch allegiance from the commander.

Dick misinterpreted the look. 'Yes, most attractive, I assure you,' he said heartily.

'I'll bear that in mind,' said Mandy even more musingly. Somewhere, in the snow-covered wastes of Siberia, a wandering wolf stopped in its tracks, cocked its ear and lifted its muzzle in a howl to the leaden sky.

Dick shuddered. 'Whoops! Somebody must have walked over my grave. Anyway what are you here for?'

'Your turtle,' said Lindy.

'Ah yes! My turtle. Follow me.' He led them into the hall, through another of the doors and along a lino-floored passage. He continued the conversation as he walked. 'I mentioned it to a friend of mine at the university and he's sending out a colleague of his, a palaeontologist, to take a look at it.'

'That's nice. We just want to have a look at it for the historical exhibition. It's going to be the centrepiece.'

'It's probably new to science, you know. If it is, it'll be named after the village and this place will become famous all over the world.'

'Really?' said Lindy. 'A bit like the Piltdown Man?'

'Yes, except that the Piltdown jawbone turned out to be a

35

forgery.' The passage ended in a room that had probably once been the farm dairy. It was now a store-room containing some battered tea chests and piles of newspapers that were rapidly reverting to their original pulp under the onslaught of damp. 'There!' said Dick proudly.

The two women inspected the turtle. It lay solidly in the middle of the floor, its back dark and sleek with the outlines of the segments of its shell clearly visible. 'Where's its head and its legs?' asked Mandy.

'The soft bits would have been eaten up by scavengers when it died.'

'It's certainly not the sort of thing Percy Bladderwort would pick up on a picnic,' commented Lindy. 'It looks very heavy.'

'It is. Well over a hundredweight. It's solid rock.'

'It's very impressive. I'm sure everyone will be most interested in it. Would it be possible for you to deliver it? I don't think I'd have the strength to move it.'

'It would be my pleasure. I'll make out a little label to go with it, saying what it is, where it was found and who has lent it.'

'That would be very kind,' said Lindy politely. 'But there's no need to go to all that trouble. I'm pretty sure everyone would know where it came from.'

'There may be tourists around and it wouldn't surprise me if the newspapers and television people did a story on it.'

'On that lump of stone?' asked Mandy dubiously.

'Oh yes. It's not every day that a new species of animal is discovered by science. Think of the excitement if the remains of an abominable snowman or the Loch Ness monster were found.'

'Hmm,' said Lindy. 'Surely the point about those is that they're still around?'

'So might this turtle be.'

Lindy sighed. 'Well, it surely won't be doing much swimming around in its present condition. Anyway, if you could bring the thing up to the church hall, I'd be very grateful.'

'It would be my pleasure. Would you like a cup of tea?'

They had a cup of tea during which Mandy generously relinquished her rights over Howard to Sweetbriar when they discovered a mutual passion for Black Forest gateau.

Dick decided to deliver the turtle the next day which was not quite what Lindy had intended as there was not yet a firm date for the exhibition and the church hall was locked. However, Dick had extra muscle in the form of Sweetbriar and Howard and they had not brought the thing all the way to the village perched on the back of a bicycle only to take it home again, so they persuaded Helga to house it underneath a bench by the wall of the public bar.

The pub became quite proud of its turtle. It lay below the deranged stag's head and gracefully accepted its role as a conversation piece. Kelvin prodded it. Flossie urinated on it. The commander barked his ankle on it as he slid hastily along the bench to avoid having to sit beside Mandy and everyone admired it except Jimmy who could not understand why there

was such a fuss about a 'girt big stone' even if it was supposed to be a 'possil'.

It stayed there until one lunchtime at the end of the week. Fridays were always busy since many of the farmers came in to boast about the deals they had made at market the previous day and they augmented the usual crowd of regulars in for their midday fix of booze and gossip. Strangers did occasionally come into the bar but they were expected, like children, to be seen and not heard, so Kelvin was understandably annoyed when one interrupted Helga while she was concentrating on pouring him a pint.

'Excuse me.'

'Wait your bloody turn, mate!' snarled Kelvin over his shoulder. He turned to look. 'Oh, sorry, miss.' The stranger was a short woman in her forties wearing thick stockings and sensible shoes with a pair of National Health glasses on her nose. Kelvin laboured embarrassedly on, much to the amusement of Jimmy who was listening in. 'I thought you were a man, you see. But I can see now that you're a lady. It's your voice. It could be either and I naturally assumed that it would be a man coming up to the bar to order drinks—'

'It just shows the danger of making assumptions,' said the woman with a tight little smile. 'I am certainly not a man and I am not here to order a drink. I'm a palaeontologist. Jessica Leach.'

Kelvin looked round the bar for a translator, but Malcolm could only come in at lunchtime once or twice a month when he played hookey from his job as an English lecturer. Kelvin played safe. 'Are you now? Very nice for you, I'm sure.'

'Does it hurt?' asked Jimmy, beginning the asthmatic wheeze which signalled a laugh. He was a devotee of bad television sitcoms.

The visitor ignored him. 'I'm here about Dick's fossil. He told me it was up here.'

'Why isn't he here himself?' asked Kelvin interestedly.

'He said he's been warned to stay at home today.'

'Warned? Did he say who by?'

'His biorhythms,' replied Jessica Leach drily.

38

'Good God!' muttered Kelvin.

'Anyway, I'd like to look at this fossil.'

'Is that what that other word meant?'

'A palaeontologist is one who studies fossils. Where is it?'

Kelvin became all action. He jumped down from his stool and cleared a way through the customers to the stag's head. 'Excuse me! Excuse me! This lady is the expert in fossils come to find out what kind of turtle ours is. Shift your backs!'

The crowds parted and many conversations were suspended so that people could hear her comments. Kelvin moved Mandy and the commander – they split in opposite directions – and slid the table out of the way so that the turtle could be clearly seen. She looked. 'Is that it?'

'Yes. Of course that's it,' replied Kelvin.

She raised her head and looked Kelvin coldly in the eye. 'You mean I have just driven thirty miles to see this?' She gestured contemptuously towards the turtle.

'Well, I'm sorry,' muttered Kelvin. He was a little indignant since he did not see that he had to apologize for anything. 'I'd've thought that it would be quite nice for a pally-thing like you to see a turtle. You don't get them round here much these days.'

Jessica Leach looked round at the patrons who were silent, sharing Kelvin's indignation. 'It's not a fossil. It's a bag of cement.' She paused for a second or two. 'If that is all, I would like you to kindly get out of my way so that I can leave this place.' Kelvin did not get out of the way, so she walked round him and through the door, slamming it hard behind her. A few flakes of plaster sloughed off the ceiling and clicked on to the tile floor.

'What did she mean, "a bag of cement"?' demanded Mandy. 'What on earth is she talking about?'

Lindy began to giggle, but put her hand over her mouth when she was sent a furious look by Kelvin. Her shoulders heaved instead. The odd snigger came from other patrons and they gradually spread round the room and turned into guffaws. Kelvin's face suddenly split in a huge grin and great cackles of laughter came out.

39

'What on earth is going on?' shouted Mandy into the uproar.

Kelvin pulled out a large red handkerchief and wiped his eyes. 'Dick's bloody biorhythms were right. If he was here, I'd kick his arse for him. It's not a fossil at all, Mandy. That old fool Percy Bladderwort must have left a bag of cement out in the rain and it went hard.' He broke off for another cackle. 'Those markings were made by the paper bag which has rotted away.'

It was one of the more memorable lunchtimes the pub had known.

Chapter Four

LINDY LABOURED long and hard over her exhibition. The fiasco of the turtle had a positive side in that the story travelled everywhere within a matter of days. Men and women, old and young, emerged blinking from the isolation of their farmsteads with photographs and artifacts that were relevant to the history of the village and pressed them into Lindy's hand. Mandy called on the commander in order to solicit contributions and, although he had hidden in a potting shed at the far end of his square patch of Brussels sprouts as soon as her 'Yoo hoo!' pierced his peaceful afternoon's weeding, she gave him a nasty turn by looming up at him in the doorway, blocking out the light, after Elfrieda had maliciously indicated where he was likely to be found. His hand had found a scallop-shaped axehead with which to ward her off and he had managed to send her away with it as an ancient relic dug out of his potato patch. He had actually looted it from a crumbling farmhouse in the Dordogne where he had stayed during a leave in 1958.

The centrepiece of the exhibition was a collection of photographs showing the local fire brigade back through the decades; the village during wartime; the genteel life of the squire's forebears, their horses and new motor cars; and village weddings with bewhiskered faces whose eyes still expressed the agony of the unaccustomed stiff collars. There were school rolls, church records, newspaper cuttings, property deeds, bits of *Domesday*, letters, bills and maps. There were artifacts – no turtle, it was true, but there was the commander's axehead, and some superb Victorian agricultural implements

41

which had been lent by a grumbling Kelvin. He had scavenged them so that he could dominate the neighbourhood after the Bomb when electricity and diesel became unobtainable. Bill produced his milk-bottle collection which covered the farms of the parish over one hundred years and even Mike Weaver, who could conjure a fifteen-pound salmon from a goldfish bowl, came up with some wicked poaching implements passed down from an ancestor who, to the eternal shame of his descendants, was caught with a stag and hanged at the next assizes. It was the catching, not the hanging, that was still shameful.

The exhibition, which was opened by Marcia, the squire's wife, was a huge success. Old people spent hours cackling over sepia photographs of church picnics, working out who was who and with whom had they done what in the years that had followed. Dusty old scandals whose protagonists had lain comfortably in the graveyard together for decades were gleefully resurrected as were ancient arguments about boundaries and deals that had gone wrong.

The village was really rather tickled to discover that it had a history. It had heard that it had, but it had never before seen

42

it clearly laid out. The pub, which itself featured in the exhibition unchanged since the dawn of photography, talked long and proudly about it. The locals often felt, but never articulated, a feeling of inferiority when faced with the worldly wisdom of the incomers. People like the commander had sailed the seven seas and Malcolm and Stephanie Jarrett had been to university. But there were Morchards, Weavers, Loosemires, Carters, Mowbrays and Bagginses in the photographs. Their descendants were the insiders, the inheritors of this bit of the country and the incomers, for all their knowledge, experience and sophistication, could never become part of its fabric as were the natives.

The exhibition was supposed to last a week but it lingered on. It was the village's equivalent of the mouldering copies of *Burke's* and *Debrett's* that filled a shelf in the squire's library.

Leon Wolff was a significant strand in the past of the village, but he was not recognized as such when he first came into the pub. He was just another seasonal tourist in his sixties who had strayed off the beaten path, more interesting than most because his clothes and his camera clearly branded him as an American even before he came up to the bar to order a drink.

Kelvin decided to speak to him, doing him a rare honour since Kelvin thought of tourists as a lion would zebra: 'Afternoon.'

'Afternoon,' replied the American. 'Nice drop of rain, this morning.'

Kelvin looked at him curiously. It was not often that one could have an intelligent conversation with a tourist, let alone with an American. He decided to test him further. 'Aye. It was the warm rain that'll keep the grass growing for a bit yet.' He cocked an inquisitive eyebrow but the American did not miss a beat.

'Not too much, though. Good open autumn. That's what's needed.'

Kelvin smiled his appreciation, thrusting out his hand. 'My name's Kelvin Morchard.'

The tourist looked delighted, shaking Kelvin's gnarled paw

with enthusiasm. 'Leon Wolff. Did I do it right? Gee! I thought I would have forgotten. It's been so long!'

'Buy the man a drink, Commander,' ordered Kelvin. 'What do you mean, "do it right"?'

'Speaking the language. It took me months to get the hang of it.'

'He's already got a drink,' observed the commander.

'Well, buy him another.'

'You buy him another,' replied the commander churlishly.

Leon Wolff held up a placating hand, his eyes dancing with pleasure. 'No, I don't want a beer. I never could stand the stuff. You guys are just the same as ever.'

Kelvin had no idea what the visitor was talking about. 'What are you talking about?'

'I've been here before. I used to drink in this pub forty years ago. It's exactly the same.'

'The same? It's not the same.' Kelvin indicated a table by the wall – that which had concealed the turtle. 'That table was only put there six years ago and the walls were painted for the Queen's Jubilee. It was the Jubilee, wasn't it, Bill?'

'That's right. They were painted for the Coronation, too, weren't they, Jimmy?'

'They were painted, yes. But I think they were painted in the same colour that they were before. Forty years ago. You must have been one of the Americans?'

'That's right. I was at the hall for six months during the war.'

'You were in the chicken house?'

'Yes. I was a driver there.' The chicken house, which now housed the communards, had been half nursing home and half R&R centre for Americans who were suffering from battle fatigue. The men of the village had been less than sympathetic as its patients had all been fresh young soldiers fatigued not by shellfire but by their training. The GIs had spread their dollars around like fertilizer on a field. Where they spread their fertilizer, they also tended to sow their seed as well. This was less often talked about since an embarrass-ingly high percentage of the sons and daughters of the parish

44

now entering middle age bore no resemblance to their putative fathers.

'I don't remember you. When exactly was that?' asked Kelvin.

'The spring of '44.'

'Ah! No wonder you don't remember him, Kelvin,' said Jimmy, making a serious social gaffe. Some topics were taboo. During that spring the War Agricultural Committee had decided that Kelvin was not farming as effectively as the nation required. A farmer from a neighbouring parish had been told to do a better job while Kelvin worked in a sawmill thirty miles away. It was six months before he got his land back and the community tacitly agreed that such an embarrassing episode should never be mentioned again.

There was an awkward silence during which Kelvin turned crimson. It was broken by the commander who, of course, knew nothing of Kelvin's shame as it happened decades before his arrival in the village. 'Did you come here often, Mr Wolff?'

'A couple of times a week. When I wasn't dating one of the girls.'

'I don't think we'd better go into that,' said Bill grimly.

'You were one of the darts players, weren't you?' asked Jimmy.

'You remember!' said Leon.

'How could I forget!' Jimmy turned to the commander. 'There were half a dozen of them who thought they could play darts! We took pint after pint off them. It was wonderful!'

'Hitler's war. Golden days,' sighed Leon Wolff. 'We were all young then – most of us, anyway.' Jimmy had obviously not been young since the Great War.

'You survived the war?' asked Ivor politely.

'Yes. I made master sergeant.'

'Like Bilko,' contributed the commander. 'No doubt you got lots of medals?'

'Oh, sure. But that was a long time ago. I'm in stationery now. I was over here on business with a couple of days to kill and I thought I'd come down here.'

'Stationery? Writing paper and things?' asked Kelvin.

45

'That's right. I've got my own business in Chicago.'

'You're rich, I imagine?'

'Well, let's say I pay my taxes and don't complain.'

'And what are you going to do now you're here?'

'Just go round old haunts and recall old memories.'

'Where are you going to stay?'

'I'll work something out.'

'There ain't a hotel round here, you know,' said Kelvin.

'I'll stay at a breakfast establishment, then. It'll only be for one night.'

'You can stay with us,' said the commander. 'Elfrieda would love it. I visited New Orleans once on a destroyer. Met a chap called Lucius. Or was it Lucien? Doesn't really matter. Anyway you will stay?'

'Thank you very much.'

There was an amiable pause in the conversation. 'I wonder what happened to all the girls? There was one real doll. She must be an old lady by now.'

'That was Mary Yerbury,' said Kelvin reverently. 'She married one of your lot and moved to America. To a place called Bullock.'

'It was Buffalo,' corrected Bill.

'That's right – Mary. She was too rich for my blood. I had one special girl. But I'm darned if I can remember her name.'

'It's probably just as well,' said Bill.

'Oh, I don't know,' argued Kelvin. 'It would be quite nice for you to meet her again.'

'She was a cutie. She had a real ass on her.'

'So one would have imagined,' commented the commander drily.

'Where did she live?' asked Kelvin.

'On one of the farms. Down a long lane.'

'That cuts it down', replied Kelvin sarcastically. 'Virtually every girl had a Yank and lived on a farm.'

'And Mary Yerbury is the only one of them who moved out,' warned Bill. 'I think you'd well let it lie.'

'Oh, stop fussing!' replied Kelvin. 'It was forty years ago! Where's the harm in it?'

'There are some things from forty years ago that are best let alone. You ought to know that, Kelvin,' warned Jimmy.

'Look, forget it,' said Leon Wolff. 'If it's going to cause trouble, I'll leave it. She'd look like my old lady now, anyway – sixty-five, 200lbs and with a temper like a wolverine.'

Kelvin chuckled. 'She sounds like Lily Baggins and it's hard to think that she could have broken hearts in her youth.'

'Perhaps ... er ... Mr Wolff's girl friend was Lily Baggins?' suggested the commander. 'Had she an American?'

'They all bloody did,' growled Jimmy.

'Lily Baggins?' said Leon Wolff, wrinkling his brow behind the metal struts of the spectacles that crossed the bridge of his nose. 'I don't think that was her name.'

'Could well have been,' grunted Kelvin. 'I remember when that sanctimonious old fart used to sell nylon stockings in the market. And you lot didn't give those away for praying in church.'

Ivor, ever the diplomat, changed the subject. 'You must go and visit the exhibition in the church hall while you're here. There's quite a lot about the war. And I'm sure the communards wouldn't mind if you looked round the hall.'

'The communards? Like communists?'

'If they're anything at all.'

'I've never met a communist,' said Leon cautiously.

'Well, you'll be able to live a little, won't you?'

Leon Wolff stayed with the commander that night, saw round the commune next morning, the exhibition in the afternoon and presented the commander with a case of whisky as he departed to catch a London train in the evening. But he left a delicate situation behind him which arose from his tour of the exhibition. It had been highly successful as a £20 note had been stuffed by him into an empty vase which had been placed fortuitously on a table by the door – but he had done some recognizing. If Lily Baggins had not been minding the door at the exhibition, all would have been well.

Many old people had lent treasured artifacts and documents on condition that the exhibition would always be manned to prevent hordes of urban vandals descending on the church hall to rob and pillage. Mrs Baggins knew all about the American visitor and she knew all about Kelvin's description of her in the pub the previous night. She also knew something else.

Mrs Baggins pounced while the commander and Leon Wolff were absorbed in pictures of the Great Flood, an event which had occurred when the river had celebrated what the experts described as 'a hundred-year event' by rising gently and inexorably a full ten feet above its normal level. 'Have you seen the photographs over there?'

'I bet you're Lily Baggins,' said Wolff with a grin.

She peered at him suspiciously, the bright smile dying on her lips. 'I didn't know you, did I?'

'No.'

'Well, how did you know my name?'

'Mr Morchard – Kelvin – described you in the bar last night.'

'He did, did he? I heard about that.'

'No, no. I said at the time that you sounded just like my wife and it's true.'

'Oh. What's your wife like?'

'Just like you.'

Lily Baggins thought for a second. Honesty was one of her few qualities. Her eyes narrowed. Even Kelvin, normally as sensitive to the moods of another as a Chieftain tank, would have realized that her expression boded ill for him. 'There's a picture of me with the choir picnic before the war. Come and see if I looked like your wife then.' Any anticipatory excitement that the invitation may have triggered in the commander and Wolff was overwhelmed by the ferocity of the scowl on her face. They both hesitated. 'Well, come on, then!' Mrs Baggins beckoned at them. They exchanged glances before reluctantly following her to the section on church activities which was laid out on a table beneath the window. Mrs Baggins pointed to a photograph bearing a label beneath proclaiming that it was the 1939 choir outing.

Leon Wolff looked briefly at the line of girls in cotton

dresses, men in jackets and flat caps and the solemn children with shorts covering their kneecaps. 'Very nice,' he commented, straightening up.

'Well? Which one is me? Did I look like your wife then?'

'I didn't notice,' replied Wolff unhappily. 'Why don't you point yourself out to me?'

'Look properly!'

The commander gave Wolff a nod to spur him on. Local women were best humoured.

Leon Wolff shrugged his shoulders, bent over the photograph again and looked properly. He even ran his index finger along the row of faces. His finger stopped. 'Hey! That one was my girl!' He looked up excitedly at the commander. 'The one I was telling you about last night! What's her name? What happened to her?'

The commander moved to the table. 'I don't suppose it can do much harm. You'll be off in an hour or two.' He looked down at the face underlined by Wolff's finger. He sighed and took his spectacles from his pocket, placing them on his nose before raising his eyebrows to peer down again. 'I've no idea who that is,' he said, shaking his head. 'She's quite pretty, though.'

'She sure was. Would you know who she is, Mrs Baggins?'

Mrs Baggins sniffed. 'There wasn't any point in asking him,' she said, jerking her head towards the commander. 'He's not local. Let's have a little look.' Her finger went down alongside that of the American. 'That's me at the end, there. I was a soprano, you know. I bought that dress for 12s 6d. Your girl—' she moved her finger along '—that's Ruth Snow.'

'Ruth Snow! That was it. How could I forget? Snow, like her skin!'

'Who is she?' asked the commander.

'Was, I'm afraid. She died nearly twenty years ago,' replied Mrs Baggins. 'She was Bill's half-sister.'

'Oh, that's a real shame!' said Leon Wolff.

'It comes to us all. Some are just taken sooner than others. She had a peaceful end. Her heart gave out when she was chasing a heifer from her garden.'

The commander looked relieved. 'Well, that's that, then.'

'Yeah, I suppose so. She was a real doll, though.' The American gave a final sad look at the picture. 'It's probably just as well. If she'd been around, it would have either spoiled my memory of her or we'd still have something going. It was a real shame when we were shipped out. We only got twenty-four hours' notice.'

The commander cast a puzzled look at Mrs Baggins who had retired to her chair by the door with a satisfied expression on her face. There was something he had missed about the last minute or two, but he could not see what it was. He shrugged, dismissing the problem from his mind. 'If you've got to catch a train, Leon, you'll have to think about going soon.'

'OK. I'll just take a few pictures of the village. I've told them back home so much about this place that they'll want to see it.'

50

'I bet you didn't tell them everything.'

'Well, no,' admitted Wolff with a smile. 'Ruth I kept to myself.'

It was quiet in the pub during the early part of that evening. The click of the latch, the squeak of the hinges, the hiss of damp logs and the laboured, uneven tick of the wall clock were the dominating sounds as the few customers supped their drinks quietly, waiting to see what the evening might bring. There was always someone who would come in whose day had contained some incident or experience that would be worthy of discussion. The clientele was usually entirely male at that hour as the women were either preparing their menfolk's supper or washing up after it. It was the commander who started the ball rolling. He came in, rubbing his hands briskly together, his nervous energy stirring the peaceful apathy of those already there.

'What are you so cheerful about?' asked Malcolm.

'Leon Wolff,' replied the commander. 'I've just seen Mick and he's delivering a case of scotch in payment for my giving Wolff a bed for the night.'

'Huh!' grunted Bill sourly. 'They haven't changed. That's the way they'd win people over back in the old days.'

'Oh yes!' exclaimed the commander. 'He found out who his girlfriend was. It was your late sister, Ruth Snow.'

Bill's jaw dropped. 'Ruth! It couldn't have been. I mean, she was always as quiet as a mouse. If it had been one of her sisters, I might have believed it, but not Ruth. She never went out with a Yank. She couldn't have done.'

'Wolff identified her in a photograph in the church hall. He was very certain about it.'

'Nonsense! How would he have known it was her?'

'Lily Baggins. She was on the door and she was in the picture too.'

'Lily Baggins!' exclaimed Bill. 'Yes, she was always a friend of Ruth when they were young.' He paused for a moment. Then he grinned. 'Well, I'll be buggered. Ruth. Who would have believed it?'

51

Jimmy, sitting in his chair in the corner of the bar, began to wheeze with laughter.

'What's the joke?' asked the commander. 'Malcolm, what's so funny?'

'Don't ask me,' replied Malcolm.

The door clicked and squeaked to announce Kelvin who walked to his usual stool and watched while Helga poured out his pint. Bill and Jimmy were still grinning at each other. Kelvin glanced at them and then looked more carefully. 'What's the joke then?'

'Nothing, nothing,' responded Bill hastily.

Kelvin turned to the commander who spread out his hands apologetically. 'I don't know what's funny. I was just telling them about Leon Wolff's old girlfriend. Lily Baggins—'

'Lily Baggins!' Kelvin gave a great guffaw and slapped his hand down on the bar. 'I thought it might have been her. It must have scared the shit out of him! What happened?' He looked eagerly at the commander, his eyes dancing with delight.

'No, his girlfriend wasn't Lily Baggins. It was Bill's sister, Ruth Snow. He saw her in a photograph in the exhibition and Lily Baggins said who it was.' The commander, in spite of his reservations at gossip on this level, could not help smiling at Kelvin's glee.

Kelvin's eyes shuffled to a halt. 'Ruth Snow? What are you talking about?'

'It was Ruth Snow that was his girlfriend. She was in a picture of a pre-war church picnic. Lily was there as well.'

'It can't have been Ruth Snow,' said Kelvin decisively.

'It was,' insisted the commander. 'Leon Wolff remembered her name. Snowy, like her skin, was what he said.'

Bill and Jimmy caught each other's eye and creased up with laughter. The commander looked at them with some bewilderment. It was not that funny. 'I've had a feeling that I've been missing something about your sister's little romance.'

'I've a feeling I can guess what,' said Malcolm. 'Reader, she married him.'

'I beg your pardon?' said the commander.

52

'It's a quotation.'

The commander showed his irritation. 'For Christ's sake, will someone tell me what the big secret is?'

'The woman may have been born Ruth Snow, but she died Ruth Morchard,' said Kelvin. 'She was my bloody wife, God rest her soul.'

Enlightenment dawned. 'Oh, I see! That explains why Lily Baggins was so keen that Wolff looked at the photograph. She must have known about the romance at the time.' Astonishment crossed the commander's face as he thought about it. 'If you lot didn't know about it, Lily Baggins must have kept it a secret for nearly forty years! That's amazing!'

'Good old Ruth!' said Bill. 'She had a bit of a life after all. What was it that Yank said? Cute little bum, wasn't it?'

'Do you mind!' objected Kelvin. 'You're talking about my missus.' He creased his forehead. 'I never noticed that she had a cute bum.'

'You wouldn't have noticed if she'd had no bum at all!' said Jimmy.

'Well, you couldn't have ever described her as a woman that'd you'd really notice,' said Kelvin defensively. 'But she was a good worker.'

'Yes, she was a good worker. Her harvest loaf was always a real picture,' agreed Bill. 'And she brought up your Prudence the same way. Milking, is she?'

'Feeding the young stock, by now,' said Kelvin, taking a sip from his beer. 'You know, I don't really mind about Ruth. Not now she's been dead all these years. I might have had something to say if she'd still been around. But not now.'

'That's a very fair attitude,' said Jimmy, peeling the stub of a hand-rolled cigarette from his bottom lip.

'It is,' agreed the commander. 'But why has it been such a secret? I mean, you know how hard it is to keep a secret round here.'

'Beats me,' said Jimmy.

'It's funny when you think about it,' mused Kelvin. 'You live in a house with someone for twenty years and you can still learn something about them.'

53

'You're wife's been dead for twenty years too?' asked Malcolm thoughtfully.

'Yes. I suppose it's an anniversary or something.'

'That's forty years ago that you got married?'

Kelvin glanced at Malcolm sardonically. 'Christ! You're quick this evening.'

What was stirring in the recesses of Malcolm's brain began to do the same in the commander's. 'When was it that the Americans were here?'

'Forty years ago, of course. That Yank said so last night,' answered Jimmy. 'Oh!' he added quietly.

Kelvin twigged too and rounded on Jimmy. 'Here! What are you trying to say?' Jimmy did not answer immediately, so Kelvin did it for him. 'You're saying that my Ruth was walking out with that Yank just before she married me!'

'I didn't say anything of the sort,' replied Jimmy.

'Yes, you bloody did!'

Bill intervened. 'Look, don't get all in a lather. It should be fairly easy to work out what was going on. When did you get married, Kelvin?'

'That's easy enough. It was the January when that two-headed calf was born at West Barton.'

'That was 1944,' said Jimmy.

There was a short silence. 'I'm not sure that gets us very far,' contributed the commander awkwardly. 'The Americans would have all left round about D-Day which was June that year. But for heaven's sake! You'd have surely known about it if she'd been seeing him. I mean, it was the first six months of your marriage!'

'I had to go away for a while round about then,' replied Kelvin, looking into his glass.

'You! Go away! I never heard that you'd lived anywhere else than on your farm!' exclaimed Malcolm.

'It was the war,' replied Kelvin evasively.

'What? Are you saying you were in the army?'

'Not exactly. Some of us who did our bit are still not allowed to talk about it.'

Malcolm snorted derisively. 'Kelvin, come on! You're not

54

saying you were parachuted into France to show the Resistance how to lay a hedge or something?'

Bill stirred on his stool. Kelvin, for all his faults, was his brother-in-law while Malcolm was nobody. He had come from somewhere like Dorset or Dorking. 'You leave Kelvin alone. Your generation wouldn't be here if it wasn't for ours.' Malcolm wisely did not argue.

'Anyway,' said the commander briskly, 'it's all history, now. And Leon Wolff is probably halfway across the Atlantic on his way back to his wife. Even if your Ruth did have a bit of a fling all those years ago, she was obviously a good wife to you and gave you a fine daughter.'

'I suppose that's true,' admitted Kelvin.

'You were quite right, by the way,' continued the commander, deciding that it was time that the subject was changed. 'He guessed who Mrs Baggins was after your description – actually she wasn't too happy about that.'

'Serve the old bag right!' replied Kelvin. There was a short silence before Kelvin's evening proceeded to deteriorate further.

'How old is Prudence, now?' asked Jimmy.

'Prudence?' repeated Kelvin. 'I dunno. I suppose she must be getting on a bit. She can't be far short of forty. It's funny to think of her as middle-aged.'

Jimmy broke into a fit of coughing as a mouthful of beer went down the wrong way. The others looked fearfully at their drinks, the floor and the walls. Nobody dared catch another's eye. 'Forty,' repeated Kelvin slowly. 'Jesus!'

The commander glanced up from his study of a slug trail that glistened on the edge of the carpet by the window. Kelvin was being wracked by an emotional maelstrom, as powerful as on the occasion when he had dropped a bottle of whisky on the pavement outside the post office. The commander cleared his throat nervously. 'Look, Kelvin. Don't jump to conclusions.'

'Absolutely!' agreed Bill vigorously. 'Ruth would never have done that. It's ridiculous to think otherwise.'

Jimmy nodded his head in assent, showering cigarette ash over his immediate environment. 'Quite. Your Ruth was a

55

good woman. And Prudence looks just like her. It's obvious that they're mother and daughter.'

'When's Prudence's birthday?' asked Malcolm. 'That might help clear things up.'

'It's in January,' replied Kelvin. 'It always saved money as her Christmas presents did for her birthday as well.' There was a ten-second silence as fingers counted off the months.

'Well, of course, that doesn't prove anything,' said Malcolm.

'It certainly proves something since I wasn't around in April.'

Bill sighed. 'I must say it looks pretty bad.'

'Bad? It's bloody outrageous! All these years I've treated Prudence as my own and that bastard was her father all along. She's been living in my house under false pretences!'

'You can't be sure of that,' protested the commander feebly.

'Wolff! That's what her name is. Prudence Wolff! She's not a Morchard at all. It's humiliating!'

'It's not your fault, Kelvin.'

Kelvin turned savagely towards the commander. 'It's not humiliating for me, you fool. It's humiliating for her! She's been thinking all these years that I was her father and it's been a bloody American all along. She's half-foreign! She may be just Prudence but I wouldn't wish something like that on a dog! Think how it's going to make her feel! An American! And she's been working on my farm all these years, pretending she's my heir and she's not at all! She's someone else's bastard!' There was spittle flecking Kelvin's lips.

Bill looked across the bar at Kelvin with stony eyes. His stare shifted to Malcolm. 'Kelvin went away during the war because the government gave his land to someone who could farm it properly,' he said flatly.

'Here!' shouted Kelvin, aghast. 'What do you think you're doing? Do you know what you're saying?'

Bill knew. 'You're a right bastard, Kelvin! She may be Prudence Wolff but half of her is a Snow and don't you ever forget it. If you don't treat her right, she'll walk out on you and then where would you be? She does all the work.'

'I'm not denying that she's got her good points. But she's

not got any claims on me. Not if she's not my daughter. She's got no rights to my farm. Not now.'

'She's legally your daughter, Kelvin. That's the law if you and your wife were married when she was born,' said Malcolm.

'Look! That Wolff is her father. She's not going to get Morchard land. That farm's been in the family too long for it to be given away to a Yank.'

'There's something else,' piped up Jimmy. 'That Yank was rich. He had a business and he gave the commander a case of whisky. If Prudence is his daughter, she'll probably inherit from him.'

That was something Kelvin had not considered and his eyes showed sudden torment.

Bill turned the knife. 'That's a very good point, Jimmy. Prudence'll probably be left a great deal of money. He virtually said he was a millionaire. Prudence could well become a millionaire herself.'

Kelvin's brow furrowed as he weighed this information. 'But he's gone back to America and he doesn't know anything about it.'

'There can't be many Leon Wolffs who own stationery businesses in Chicago,' Bill chuckled. 'I think this might be Prudence's lucky day after all. With her own money she'll be able to buy her own farm. She might even move to America.'

'Move to America? said Kelvin. 'She couldn't walk out on me – not after all I've done for her over the years.' Kelvin was not one of Nature's blood donors. Instead he was one of those rare people with incorruptible integrity. His every action was ruled by self-interest. If he had been clever enough to be able to conceal it, he could have succeeded in any sphere of human activity.

'For heaven's sake!' exclaimed the commander. 'I thought you were going to cast her out into the snow five minutes ago!'

'But that was before I found out that she was going to be rich. Do you really think he would give her money?'

The commander sighed. He had known Kelvin for only five years and could not believe that he understood him. 'If you

57

are prepared to cut her off after forty years because she's not your daughter, by the same strange logic he will acknowledge her.'

'Bloody hell! If Prudence became a millionaire, think what I could do with the money! I could buy a new tractor! Or start having racehorses like you used to, Bill.'

'Don't forget, it would be Prudence who would become the millionaire, not you,' warned Jimmy.

'She's my own daughter! Well, she isn't of course, but you know what I mean. She'll see her old father right after all I've done for her. Anyway, I'm in charge of the money in my household and it's me who decides what's to be done with it!'

'She'll run her own life!' said the commander. 'She's a forty-year-old woman!'

The conversation had been so engrossing that the clock had ticked on and the fire had kept hissing without anyone taking any notice. More importantly, the latch also clicked and the hinges had creaked.

'Who's a forty-year-old woman?' queried Lindy, coming up to the bar.

'Prudence,' replied Jimmy before the men could close ranks on this delicate subject.

'Balls! She's thirty-eight. She was born in 1946.'

'What?' shouted Kelvin. 'She's forty. We worked it out. She was born in 1944, the year of the two-headed calf.'

'The one at West Barton? That was 1946 too. There's a newspaper cutting about it in the exhibition. Anyway, I know she's thirty-eight. I had her medical card out when I gave her a tetanus booster last week.'

Kelvin's expression slowly turned to one of great anguish. 'That's not fair. If she's only thirty-eight, she won't be a millionaire.'

'What are you talking about, Kelvin?' asked Lindy.

'We thought that she and that American . . .' his voice trailed into silence. 'Shit!' he said savagely.

'You are a stupid bugger, Kelvin,' said Bill into the heavy silence which followed. 'Lindy, may I buy you a drink?'

58

Chapter Five

IT WAS NOT just that Frank Mattock was rich that made him unusual in the parish – there were plenty of farmers whose land could have been realized for impressive sums of cash – but the fact that he had made his money himself. He made it obvious enough by clanking round the neighbourhood weighed down with gold bangles and chains which advertised his presence by winking and flashing in the sunlight as he drove his pedigree Holsteins between the fields of his ample farm. However, the village was surprised when he decided to enter the property business by buying up the old tithe barn that stood near the church.

It was not a tithe barn to thrill the shade of Pevsner: there were no massive stone walls or buttresses or hammer-beam roof. It was a more modest brick and timber structure befitting the few bushels of oats and barley that the surrounding parishes grudgingly yielded to the Almighty's servants at harvest time. It had recently been used to store five-gallon plastic drums, originally containing formic acid silage additive, which the parish council had decided would be ideal to use for distributing water during the frequent occasions when the village supply failed. They had been there for nearly six years, gathering layers of dust and mouse turds while the acrid stench from their interiors, in spite of frequent rinsing during the early months, still had the power to rouse a well-swooned Victorian maiden lady at a hundred paces.

At first it was assumed that Frank had bought the barn to expand his agricultural empire. There was some concern at this since he was not the most environmentally conscious of farmers. Butterflies faltered in their flight, stalled and spun to the ground when they crossed a hedge into the airspace above his land, because Frank believed in chemicals and saturated his acres with fungicides, pesticides and herbicides. The pub was not happy.

'What I'd like to know is what he's going to keep in there,' said the commander. He had wedged himself into a corner of the bar where Mandy could not get to him.

'Poisons of some kind, I expect,' muttered Malcolm.

'It'll be chickens. Lots and lots of smelly chickens,' replied Kelvin, who was quite happy at the prospect since he lived well out of the village. 'I've heard Frank say that he's often thought of going into intensive egg production.'

'Oh, that sounds quite nice, doesn't it, Commander?' said Mandy. 'It's nice to have a few chickens around. Mummy used to keep some during the war.' The other patrons looked at her speculatively. The idea of Mandy having a mummy and a childhood seemed rather incongruous. She ought to have sprung into existence, already lipsticked and eye-shadowed, out of a Christmas cracker and given a bollocking to all present at her incarnation for leaving the dirty pudding plates around.

'I think Frank was thinking in terms of thousands of chickens,' said Kelvin.

'The more the merrier,' responded Mandy gaily. 'The clucking is so soothing.'

'Stupid cow!' growled Jimmy, who could afford to be rude to anyone as he was protected by the armour of seventy-five years. 'Hens shit, and it makes catshit smell like lavender. Clucking indeed!' He took a gulp from his pint of bitter, dribbling a little on to his khaki shirt front.

'He'd need planning permission and it'd have to come before the parish council,' said the commander. 'He won't find it easy to fill the village with chickens.'

'How clever of you to think of that!' cried Mandy. 'We're so lucky to have you on the council to protect us!' The latch on the door of the pub clicked up and the door squeaked open. Mandy rolled her eyes like a ventriloquist's dummy. 'Talk of the devil!' she whispered hoarsely as it opened to admit Frank.

He looked carefully round the pub, checking on who was present before moving to the bar and ordering a lager. Mandy looked covetously at the sovereign ring on his little finger. Frank had never really become part of the agricultural mafia of which Kelvin, Bill and Ivor were such stout members. It may have been that he was too young, still barely forty, or it may have been that he was too flashy, both in his dress and in his farming. The non-farming element in the village thought it was because he knew what he was doing. The others farmed by the seat of their pants, doing as they had always done and secure in the knowledge that a cow had been a cow and a grain of barley had been a grain of barley since before they were born and would remain so when they were naught but dust.

Frank did not have the same faith. He read books and magazines, discussed innovations with technical advisors and knew that the scrubby little shorthorns his father had chopped up in the back of the family butcher's shop which had gone out of business in the mid-fifties were very different creatures from his lanky, milk-gushing Holsteins.

'How much did you pay for the tithe barn, Frank?' asked Kelvin.

'£8,000,' Jimmy answered for him, scornful that Kelvin had to ask. 'What are you going to do with it?'

'You know that it is highly unlikely that the parish council will give permission for an intensive chicken unit so close to the centre of the village, don't you?' said the commander.

Frank took a long pull at his pint. 'So you reckon that I'd have difficulty with permission for chickens, Commander? Perhaps I should build a house next to the barn instead. Would I get permission for that?'

'A house? You want to build a house?' The commander burbled on for a bit as he and everyone else assessed the implications if Frank built a house. How much would it cost? What would he do with it? What could he sell it for? Think of the profit he could make! 'Oh dear! A house? Why should you want to build a house?'

'There could be a bob or two in it eventually. Or I could use it to house a farmworker.'

'You haven't got a farmworker,' objected Kelvin.

'I might need a cowman soon. What do you think, Commander?'

'There could be problems about it. Wouldn't you agree, Ivor?'

'There certainly would be,' put in Kelvin. 'Can't go building houses all over the place. Not with the sewers we've got in the village. When I was on the council, I used to complain about them regularly.'

'But you resigned, didn't you?' said the commander acidly. 'Another problem I can see is the preservation of the barn. We've got precious few old buildings left as it is. What with the sewers and worries about our heritage, I'd be very surprised if the council would give its permission.'

'Oh well. It wouldn't much matter. I was just wondering. It's chickens that I'll be doing,' said Frank.

'I've already said that chickens will be definitely out.'

'So you say, Commander. But I've had a word with a couple of district councillors and they said there'd be no problem. They said I wouldn't need any permission anyway because it's not a change of use. It's been an agricultural building for centuries and I intend that it should remain one – with 10,000 chickens inside.'

'You wouldn't dare!' exclaimed the commander. 'It would stink the village out!'

'It would, I know,' agreed Frank earnestly. 'That's why I just thought of putting up a house instead. It would be better for the community.'

'I think a house would be an excellent idea, under the circumstances,' said Malcolm.

Frank winked at him. 'Oh well,' he sighed, 'I suppose I may just have to settle for that.'

Kelvin and the commander had suspicions that they had been outmanoeuvred, but Jimmy and everyone else had been too concerned about being blighted by the miasma of hens to afford to indulge in the luxury of keeping Frank in his place.

'That's very good of you, Frank,' said Jimmy earnestly. 'There aren't enough people in this community who think of their fellow men.'

'Amen to that!' agreed Maud fervently. Her post office was near to both the church and the barn.

'Good,' said Frank. 'Mandy, is Keith very busy at the moment?'

'Over here, Frank,' said Keith, waving his hand. He was sitting beneath the stag's head. Most regulars avoided that bench as the stuffed head made them uneasy. Over the years its skin had withered back from the glass eyes to give it a manic glint as if it contemplated a spring from its hook to tear the throat out of any drinker who came too close. In the shadow of the twin threats of the decorporated stag and his wife, Keith was even more self-effacing than usual.

Frank walked over, pulling an envelope from the inside of his yellow anorak. 'I'd like you to take a look at this, Keith. It's a picture of the house I'd like to put up. I was wondering if you might have a look at it. I'll be wanting a builder and I think you've done a great job on your own house.' He handed over the paper. 'Let me know what you think of it.' He drained his glass, placed it on the bar, gave a tight smile to the commander and left, slamming the door behind him. The latch clicked down into the silence a few seconds later.

'Well, bugger me!' said Kelvin, expressing the general view. 'Who'd have thought it? He wanted to stick up a house all the time! But he must be off his rocker to ask Keith to build it!'

'What do you mean? Keith is a wonderful builder. Frank said he did a lovely job on our cottage and he's been very busy since then,' flared Mandy.

'But we couldn't have places like that all over the village, could we?'

'Why ever not? "Pixie's Bower" is a lovely cottage. It always looks a real picture, doesn't it, dear?' She nudged her husband who grunted acknowledgement from Frank's sheet of paper in which he was absorbed.

'It's a bit bigger than our cottage,' he said.

'Let's have a look,' said Kelvin.

63

'Bring it up to the bar where we can all see,' ordered the commander, clearing towels and ashtrays from the surface in front of his stool. Keith handed over the piece of paper and the commander spread it out on the warped and ancient oak of the bar. 'Heavens!' he murmured, after he had placed his reading glasses on his nose.

Kelvin peered and sucked in his breath with indignation.

'Cowman's cottage indeed! We can't have a place like this in the village. Who the hell does Frank think he is?'

'JR! That's who he thinks he is!' cried Mandy, making the commander start nervously as she placed her cheek close to his so that she could see. 'That's a picture of "South Fork". In *Dallas*.'

'A swimming pool right next to the churchyard is out for a start,' contributed Malcolm grimly. 'And he's not going to be allowed to knock down the barn.'

'The best thing to do is work out what we'll let him put up at the next council meeting,' suggested the commander. 'Something small that is in keeping with the traditions of the community. Something more appropriate for a cowman.'

'Something that he'll find difficult to sell to a weekender,' added Kelvin.

'Well, just so long as you don't make it too complicated,' warned Keith.

Contractors who build in cities can erect great sheets of plywood to hide their work and their mistakes from the prying eyes of the passers-by. The contract for Frank's house, although one of the largest feats of civil as opposed to agricultural engineering that had taken place in the village for a decade, did not stretch to such luxuries. Most inhabitants of the parish made sure they passed the site at least once each day.

It was something different. The scenery varied anyway with the passing of the seasons. Leaves appeared on the creeper which enveloped the church tower, only to drop off six months later. The single sunflower that Jimmy grew annually in his front garden was always something at which eyes attuned to

64

daisies and dandelions could marvel, while the gradual decomposition of his Ford Consul, which he had ceased driving five years earlier, could be closely followed from year to year.

However, there had never been anything like Frank's house. It was an intoxicating luxury and the villagers made the most of it. They did not merely eye it as they walked past. They walked round it, over it, through it with critical or appreciative eyes and passed advice, criticism and comment on its construction. The village took the house to its collective heart. Designed by the parish council, which had been Frank's intention all along, it was a square concrete box constructed from building blocks which represented the community's triumph over the threat of chickens. Some even saw it as a leap into the twentieth century. It was not every

village round about that could boast an example of modern architecture in its midst.

Under the eyes of the village, trucks came to deliver sand, cement, blocks and concrete. Drains went in, concrete was poured, and scaffolding rose. Everyone was entranced. Keith was a hero in the pub. This was no mere single-span concrete barn – all the rage at the obscure end of farm lanes – but a permanent addition to their everyday lives. Everyone had a critical stake in the business and bombarded Keith with advice. It was the commander who observed that there was no provision for a window in the bathroom and at 10pm helped Keith to pull down the blocks necessary to make a hole just as the mortar was setting. It was Dick who volunteered to monitor the wellbeing of the bats that lived in the tithe barn which almost kissed gables with the new house. It was Mrs Baggins who bustled through the front door of her cottage next to Jimmy's across the lane with two mugs of tea and two rich tea biscuits twice a day to give comfort to the workers.

There was one problem. The building inspector had been used to making a pleasantly moon-lit income by preparing plans for barns and house extensions on his patch for submission to the council. Frank had not needed his services and he was not happy about it.

The man dropped in shortly after the roof had gone up. Keith was away collecting some wood from the sawmill and had missed him and it had been up to his navvy, Jason Loosemire, to act as host and explain what had happened to Keith when he returned: 'He's not a cove I care for very much.'

'Yes,' said Keith impatiently. 'What did he say?'

'He shouted and waved his arms about for a bit when I dropped a block on his foot and then he went outside. I followed him after a minute or two when he had gone quiet and he was looking up at the roof, grinning like a Hallowe'en pumpkin. Then he went away.'

'The roof!' said Keith with alarm. 'He liked the roof! What's wrong with the roof?' He rushed out of the house, the metal on the soles of his boots denting the sap-filled wooden floors and echoing round the shell of the interior. He splashed through the mud to the lane and looked back at the roof. 'What's wrong with the roof? It looks all right. Those tiles are straight. What did he say was wrong with it, Jason?'

'He didn't say nothing was wrong with it,' shouted Jason, leaning in the doorway. 'He was just looking at it and laughing.'

'Well, why didn't you ask him about it?'

'I told you. I didn't fancy him.'

Keith looked at him in exasperation. 'What's that got to do with it? Look, have you any idea why he was laughing at the roof?'

'Not a clue. Perhaps he was happy, thinking about his bird or something. He didn't say anything so there's nothing to worry about.'

But Keith worried, although neither his client nor his peers were particularly concerned. The civil engineering projects that they were used to relied upon baler twine as their principal ingredient, followed by recycled nails and any old scraps of wood that lay around. The roof seemed fine to Kelvin who had seen an entire home-built tractor shed collapse when a bullock scratched itself on the door frame, as it also seemed to the commander whose polythene growing tunnels carpeted the surrounding countryside like great undulating slugs after the first stiff breeze of autumn.

In spite of his concern, the house cruised ahead until Malcolm Jarrett went to have a look shortly before the scaffolding was removed. On Thursday Keith and his assistant kept going until eight o'clock to give those who worked during the day an opportunity to come to look at the house while the builders modestly enjoyed the admiration and the praise. Malcolm Jarrett's admiration was not actually worth a great deal. He was not a local, which was devaluation for a start, nor had he the countryman's eye for a structure. Everyone in the country can build if they are pushed; it is not an activity confined to contractors. Malcolm was also the nearest the community had to an intellectual so could not be expected to have any sense.

67

The men were cleaning up for the day when Malcolm arrived, wearing his gumboots. 'May I have a look around, Keith?'

'Be my guest,' replied Keith with a lordly wave of his trowel. By this time the walls and roof had been completed and work was underway on the interior, but the outside of the building was still clothed in scaffolding. Malcolm walked carefully through the doorway and disappeared from view.

'Are you going to the pub tonight?' Keith asked his assistant.

'Yeah, I suppose so. You coming along?' Jason would not normally associate with Keith. Being over thirty, Keith was geriatric and many years as a Reading butcher had left great gaps in his conversation. He could not discuss the way the salmon were running up the river, whether the squire's pheasants were worth taking yet or whether it was true that you had to go out twice with Lizzie Steer before she would let you into her knickers. However, Keith both paid him and felt that it was his duty as boss always to buy the first drink.

'Yes.'

'Well, I won't have time for more than a quick one.' Jason carefully made his mark to ensure he would not have to buy back. 'Going out.'

'Going out? Lizzie Steer?'

'How did you know?' demanded Jason.

'She told me,' replied Keith innocently.

Or was it innocently? Jason looked at Keith with suspicion. Keith was just a twit. Everyone knew that. But he had recently been rumoured to be a randy twit.

Malcolm had clambered around on the scaffolding to examine the upper storey and he now reappeared at the entrance to the house. Both Keith and Jason looked at him hopefully. Even Malcolm's opinion was worth something. 'Er . . . very nice, isn't it?'

'So they say,' replied Jason stolidly.

'You don't often see fireplaces on the first floor these days.'

'The fireplaces? No, I suppose not,' responded Keith.

'Aren't the chimneys meant to go all the way through?'

'What do you mean?' said Keith. 'Of course they go all the way through.'

'One of them doesn't. The chimney from the bottom is blocked by the fireplace on the floor above.'

'Don't be silly,' replied Keith, but his voice lacked conviction and he looked furtively up and down the lane to ensure that there was nobody of importance within earshot. 'Is it really blocked?'

'Yes.'

'Jason, that was your job. What the hell have you gone and done?'

'Just what I was told.'

'You weren't bloody well told to block up the fireplace.'

'I was just following the plans. If you can't draw up proper plans, it's your fault. Yours and Frank's. You should have got that council inspector bloke to do them.'

'If it was on the bloody plan that you should jump off the roof, you wouldn't do it, would you?'

'Of course not. I'm not daft,' replied Jason.

'Well, why block up the chimney, then?'

Jason seemed confused. 'What's that got to do with jumping off the roof? There was nothing about that on the plans but the fireplace upstairs was.'

Keith turned to Malcolm in resignation. 'Modern youth!' he sighed.

'Don't you take that attitude with me, Keith,' bristled Jason. 'I don't have to work here. I'd get bloody nearly as much from the Social Security as working here.'

'You're still collecting Social Security,' responded Keith.

Jason looked triumphant. 'Exactly!' he replied.

Both Malcolm and Keith appeared puzzled. Malcolm spoke after a short pause. 'There was something else that I didn't understand—'

'Bugger the chimney for tonight,' said Keith. 'Are you coming for a drink? I'll explain what you don't understand in the pub.'

Keith was now an important figure in the pub, receiving respectful nods of greeting from the others. With Frank's gold

69

running through his economy, he quite often bought drinks for other patrons. He ordered a round and the three of them took the ritual first sip, smacking their lips with the faraway expression of men who were being men at the end of a hard day.

'What was it that you didn't understand, Malcolm?' asked Keith loudly. He was very happy with the role of advising Malcolm about the intricacies of his profession in an avuncular fashion.

'How are people going to get to the upper floor?'

'Of the house?' asked Keith, off balance at the inanity of the question.

'Yes. There aren't any stairs.'

'What?' shouted Kelvin. 'Of course there are stairs! I was up there this morning. You were with me, Commander. We were both up there.'

'Yes. That's right. We were discussing the bathroom.'

'Well, you must have climbed up the scaffolding, because there certainly aren't any stairs.'

Jason started to guffaw. 'He's right, you know. Keith forgot to put in a staircase. He's been running up and down the scaffolding and not even noticed.'

'So have you,' observed Malcolm mildly.

'Not my fault. I just work for him.'

'But you're supposed to be a builder too,' said the commander.

'Don't pick on me,' replied Jason with indignation. 'The whole bloody village has been traipsing up and down that ladder and this smart-arse is the only person to have noticed.'

Keith drained his pint and slammed it down on the counter. 'Damn!' He gave Malcolm a savage glance and stormed out of the pub.

Kelvin peered through the leaded lights of the window after him. 'He's going back to have a look at the house,' he announced.

Many of the customers in the pub walked the hundred yards to commiserate with him in this misfortune. Malcolm,

70

educated enough to know the likely fate of messengers who bore ill tidings, prudently stayed behind to chat up Helga behind the bar while Jason went off, rather nervously, to his tryst with Lizzie.

The building inspector dropped in the following week to spring his little surprise. He rubbed his hands together in pleasure as he emerged from his small, red motor car. He was a man in his mid-thirties with odd tufts of ginger hair sprouting from his cheekbones, his ears, his nostrils and above the collar of his shirt. Without clothes he would have looked like a short-armed orang-utan and he had a loud, booming voice which would have been very useful for communicating between the jungle treetops. Frank, Keith and Jason were present to respond to the 'Ho, ho, ho' which the sight of the cottage drew from him. He hummed happily as he toured the house. Keith, who had been looking forward to his visit with considerable foreboding, began to cheer up. The house was his life's masterpiece so far and he was very proud of it.

'Nice view,' commented the inspector, looking out through the living-room window at the tower of the church and the heather-purple moor that rose up beyond.

'We made up those windows ourselves,' replied Keith proudly. 'Seasoned ash. You can't buy that sort of quality off the shelf. Isn't that right?'

'Yes, they're very fine frames. Not quite what I would have specified—'

'There's nothing in regulations that says you can't use ash in windows,' interrupted Keith.

'I didn't say there was. Regulations are concerned with their size and the ceiling heights of the rooms.'

'I know all that,' replied Keith rather testily. 'And you won't be able to find anything wrong with them.'

'Oh good. Still, I always think it best to use someone who knows what he's doing when it comes to drawing up plans, don't you?'

'We knew what we were doing, didn't we Jason?'

''S'right.'

The inspector rubbed his hands together again. 'Jolly good.

71

Mistakes can get very expensive.' He measured the doorframe with his eye.

'7 feet 6 inches. Not a fraction under,' said Keith emphatically.

The inspector smiled. 'They're supposed to be a minimum of 198 centimetres.'

Keith's jaw opened and shut in horror like that of a goldfish. Frank, who had been growing more and more twitchy at the bonhomie being shown, exclaimed, 'Bugger it. I knew there'd be something.'

'However,' continued the inspector smoothly, 'you don't need to worry about that since 198 centimetres is 6 feet 6 inches.'

Keith sagged against the wall. 'You did that deliberately, you bastard.'

The inspector chuckled, his beer belly vibrating. 'You ain't seen nothing yet. Shall we go upstairs?'

'What do you mean, "ain't seen nothing yet"?' asked Frank, but the inspector merely chortled. The natives exchanged uneasy glances. It was becoming evident that he had a Damoclean sword secreted somewhere about his person, but he kept it sheathed until they got outside. His suppressed excitement was such that Frank received an inkling of what it must have been like for an aristo on his last journey in a tumbril.

The inspector stepped outside and took several deep breaths, stretching out his arms to show a length of hairy ginger wrist at the end of each sleeve. He turned round to the house, merrily whistling *The Road to the Isles* through his teeth.

'It's the roof,' groaned Keith. 'It's got to be the roof.'

'The roof?' echoed the inspector with an innocent expression on his face as he lifted his eyes heavenwards. 'What about the roof? I'm sure it will show the same high standard of craftsmanship that you say everything else displays. Yes, I thought so. It looks fine.'

'You mean there's nothing wrong with it?' asked Keith incredulously.

'Wrong with it? I don't think so.' There was a gleam in his

eye that would have made even Lucifer pause before he unlocked his molten version of the Pearly Gates. The inspector looked back at the roof. He frowned like a pantomime villain. 'Oh dear, oh dear me. I'm not so sure about that. I shall have to check the plans in the car.'

'What?' demanded Keith. 'What do you mean?'

'The roof.' The inspector pursed his lips and shook his head. 'I could be wrong, but I'd better check.' He skipped merrily over to his car in the lane, flashing a beaming smile to Jimmy who was watching the proceedings under the guise of clipping his box hedge.

'Shit!' said Frank with venom. 'What's wrong with the bloody roof? If that sod is mucking us about, I'll have him.' Jason looked at Frank with admiration, coveting his ability to make a threat that sounded so certain of execution.

The inspector returned with the plans. 'I was afraid of that.'

'What?' demanded Frank aggressively.

'Look here.' He pointed at the plans with a hirsute digit.

Both Frank and Keith looked. It was the elevation showing the new house adjacent to the barn. 'What about it?' asked Frank.

'The height.'

'Oh,' said Frank as he, Keith and Jason looked at the roof which stood a few inches above that of the tithe barn. 'I see.'

'Well, I'm damned if I do,' said Keith. 'It looks fine to me.'

'It's supposed to be exactly matching the height of the barn,' said the inspector happily.

'Well it does, just about. It may be a tiny bit high, but I don't really see that it matters very much. Anyway how was I supposed to know that?'

'You may not have known it, but it was specifically mentioned in a letter to Mr Mattock. It was something that the parish council was extremely concerned about.' The inspector's eyes were twinkling with glee. ' "Ensuring that the new cottage blended in with our heritage" was how they put it when they were consulted by the planning department.'

'I completely forgot about it,' said Frank miserably.

'Oh well,' said Keith. 'No great harm done. We're sorry

73

about it. We'll get the council to change their decision if it'll make you any happier. They don't give a damn, really.'

The inspector pursed his lips in mock dismay. 'Oh dear me. It's not that simple. You can't just change a decision of the district council when you want to. That planning agreement has the force of law.'

'What do you suggest?' asked Frank humbly.

'Me?' If he had been Miss Piggy, he would have said 'Moi?' 'There's nothing I can do. Not now. It's much too late for that. It was a mistake not to have someone properly qualified keeping an eye on things in the first place.'

'All right, all right,' said Frank. 'I'm sorry. I should have hired you. Next time I'll make sure I will. But what happens next?'

'There's only one thing that can happen. It'll have to come down.'

'That'll be a shame,' said Jason. 'That barn's been around for a long time.'

Even the mightiest jungle giant of the rain forest would have vibrated to the hoots of delight that finally burst from the inspector's lips. 'It's not the barn that's got to come down,' he gasped, retreating backwards towards his car in face of the thunder in Frank's face. 'It's the house.'

'Oh, come off it,' said Jason. 'It'd cost a fortune.'

'Yes, it will,' smiled the inspector through his car window. 'I'll send you an official letter about it.'

'Are you serious?'

'Oh yes. I'm serious all right.'

'We could lower the roof and the ceilings in the bedrooms,' suggested Frank desperately.

'Wouldn't work,' gloated the inspector. 'It's the downstairs where you've got the extra height. Seven-foot-six-inch door-ways! That's where the problems start. Bye-bye!' Chortling, he started up his car and went off down the lane.

The pub was incensed. Frank was at fault, certainly, and there was some pleasure in seeing the community's most gilded citizen with egg on his face. It was also true that the parish council had insisted upon the symmetry of roof ridges in the first place. But that was only demanded so that its members could demonstrate that they had power. A far more important principle at stake was that of local independence. It was a village matter and up to the community to sort out: no jumped-up little bureaucrat could be allowed to interfere. But the official letter came and the appeal against its findings was refused. It was very simple: if Frank wanted his house, the apex of its roof ridge must match that of the barn in height.

Chapter Six

'BURN THE barn down,' suggested Kelvin, once the doors of the pub had been firmly locked behind the few strangers who had ventured in . After 11pm, business continued until the last man out washed up any remaining glasses and locked the back door behind him as he ventured out to face the dawn chorus. 'Then there wouldn't be any barn, let alone a roof for them to worry about.'

'That would be arson,' responded Percy, the local policeman.

'But I wouldn't claim on the insurance,' said Frank.

'Percy's right. It would be illegal, somehow. Trying to subvert the democratic processes of local government, perhaps,' contributed Malcolm. 'There's got to be another way. Can't you just make the roof a bit less steep, or something?'

'I wish we could. Quite apart from the cost of ripping it down and shortening all the timbers, there are all sorts of regulations about the slope of the roof and things. And that blasted inspector will not let us get away with a thing.'

'Slip him a couple of hundred quid,' recommended Percy. 'That's all he wants. If he's any trouble in the future, then I could have him for taking bribes.'

'I tried that on the telephone and got nowhere. He said it had gone above his head, and anyway he thought it was in his interests to do me.'

'*Pour encourager les autres* to get him to draw up plans in future, I suppose. Then you'll just have to take it down to the first floor and rebuild,' said the commander, 'and put the extra cost down to experience. I remember once when I was on a courtesy visit on a frigate in Asia – bloody hot it was but the girls were quite charming. Penang, Djakarta, Bangkok. It was one of those sort of places—'

'Oh shut up!' interrupted Mandy. 'Frank, there's a much easier way of doing it. It would cost you very little too. Look at it the other way round. Instead of reducing the house, why don't you raise the barn?'

'Raise the barn? What do you mean, dear?' asked her spouse. 'It would cost just as much to rebuild the barn as to rebuild the cottage.'

'Don't be stupid, dear. You wouldn't have to do any of that. Just put a hat on it. You could do it very easily. Just raise the ridge a bit.'

There was silence while the pub thought it over. 'It wouldn't work,' said Ivor. 'He's going to examine the place with a bloody microscope.'

'He'll be examining the house, not the barn. It won't occur to him to look at its roof.'

'He will when he finds that there are no obvious changes to the house.'

'Well, don't give him time. Hassle him when he comes. Keep him off balance.'

'You know, it might just work,' said Frank, hope dawning on his face.

'I could turn up in uniform and talk about receiving information about soliciting bribes or something,' contributed Percy.

'That would scare him shitless,' said the commander gleefully. 'Mandy, you're brilliant!'

'Oh, Commander!' breathed Mandy. 'I didn't mean it when I told you to shut up just now.'

The commander backtracked hurriedly. 'Well, perhaps brilliant is putting it too strongly, but it's certainly worth a try. We could ask the squire to go along too. He's a magistrate. With him and Percy breathing heavily in the background, the man'll be in and out of the village without even turning off his car engine.'

'What do you think, Keith?' asked Frank. 'Shall we give it a go?'

'Keith will give it a go,' replied Mandy.

Keith and Jason tackled the problem with confidence. One of the difficulties that they faced was the time element. It would have taken weeks to finish the rebuilding of the house whereas it was only a matter of a day to wire some corrugated-iron roof ridges to the top of the barn once they had marinated for a week in Frank's slurry pit to encourage weathering. Then work stopped to allow a credible amount of time to pass while the scaffolding round the house was shrouded in black silage plastic, just in case the inspector happened to do some spying.

He came. The commander was helplessly ensnared in the post office by a communard in a discussion about the nature of a carrot's consciousness, but through the window he saw the inspector's red car pull up in the lane in front of the new cottage.

Jimmy, however, was on the spot. He spent most of his waking hours, when he was not in the pub, tickling and teasing the soil in his vegetable patch to ensure that he won more classes than the commander in the annual horticultural show. He straightened up, after worrying at the root of an intrusive blackthorn from the hedge that separated his garden from a neighbouring field, to see the inspector park his car and stride purposefully towards the shrouding plastic. Although he did not see the commander gesticulating in silent horror through the glass between a poster about buying TV licence stamps and a warning about the dangers of colorado beetle, Jimmy knew where his duty lay. Thinking fast, he let out a mighty cry, clutched at his heart and leaned heavily on his garden gate. The inspector hesitated for a moment, torn between his curiosity and his duty. His curiosity won and he came over to Jimmy's aid.

'Are you all right?' he asked from a distance of about six feet.

'My heart! I think I'm going.' Jimmy slumped over the mossy stone of his wall. He rolled his eyes at the inspector.

'Help me to the house. Give me your arm.'

The average man would have already been jogging up the path with the moribund senior citizen borne tenderly in his arms. But Jimmy was a most unprepossessing senior citizen. Most of the trouble came from the fact that his elderly lurcher, Patsy, slept the night upon Jimmy's clothes which lay on the floor at the bottom of his brass bed; she had been incontinent for several years.

The inspector had the wind in his face and the afternoon sun behind him and could be forgiven for being reluctant to come closer than he had to. But he had to in response to a direct request for an arm. He extended it. Jimmy grabbed it with his skinny hand. 'Gotcha!'

The inspector lurched backwards in alarm. 'Geddoff!' he yelled, but Jimmy was holding on with the determination of the Ancient Mariner.

'Trespassing!' roared Jimmy. 'I saw you! Sneaking up to someone else's property. You're a burglar! Help! Help! Someone call the police!'

'Let me go, you fool! What on earth do you think you're

doing?' The inspector was reluctant to use much force to break free since Jimmy, even if he was not having a heart attack, was a poorly preserved septuagenarian. He had the sort of body that stands by the side of busy roads asking to be helped across. If it was offered violence, it looked as if it would pack up completely and that could lead to nothing but trouble.

The inspector shook his arm, but Jimmy held on, not quite sure what he ought to do next. He essayed another 'Help!', but it lacked the conviction of his earlier utterance. However, reinforcements were on hand.

The first to come to his aid was Patsy who had been dozing peacefully on the garden path a dozen feet away. The shouts of her master had woken her, but her senses were in such poor condition that she had not been able to identify their distance or direction. She hauled herself to her feet, carefully straddled her quivering legs and concentrated as hard as she could. Jimmy's second 'Help!' gave her the clue she needed. She swivelled her grizzled greyhound muzzle like a defective radar dish and homed in, all her old instincts creaking into action. She lumbered across the lawn and, with a remarkable example of the power of positive thinking, she managed to launch herself into the air across the garden wall. Patsy's granny had been an Irish wolfhound and the inspector now saw a large grey hearthrug sailing through the air towards him with obvious hostile intent, rather like a nasty alien from an episode of *Startrek*. The dog, who was filled with exhilaration at her best leap for at least eighteen months, struck the inspector full in the chest, knocking him from Jimmy's grasp and to the ground.

The inspector was winded; so was Patsy who lay on top of him for a few seconds until she had regained her puff. Then she recalled her duty and seized the nearest portion of her victim's anatomy – his wrist – between her jaws and gummed it, growling ferociously.

'Cool!' said Jimmy, peering interestedly over the wall. 'I didn't think the old girl had it in her!'

The inspector was not quite clear what had happened to

80

him, but he knew it was bad. He heaved his body, throwing Patsy from him, his wrist sliding from between her toothless gums. She landed in a dejected heap, knowing that she had enjoyed her last foray into canine ferocity. The inspector staggered to his feet. 'You did that deliberately!' he gasped. 'You were just trying to stop me looking at that house!'

'That's right,' agreed Jimmy who was enjoying the tranquillity born of the knowledge that, whatever the ultimate outcome, he had done his bit.

'Well, it won't bloody work. They're up to something and it's my duty to find out what it is.'

'Oh no, you won't,' announced the commander, who was in a bit of a lather, having sprinted the fifty yards from the post office with the communard at his heels.

'Oh yes I will,' replied the inspector, grimly refastening his shirt buttons and tucking his hair back under cover.

'Oh no you won't. By the authority vested in me as a member of the Emergency Volunteers, I have the power to forbid you access to designated areas and I hereby invoke such powers. Under the Emergency Powers Act of 1973 you need a magistrate's warrant to enter and, if you should ignore my instructions, you can be prevented by the use of deadly force.'

'Don't be ridiculous! I don't believe there is such an act, and even if there was it would only be a £10 fine.'

'I'll have you know I used to command a Polaris submarine,' replied the commander loftily. This was not actually true, but he had known someone who did.

While the inspector tried to work out the relevance of this statement and whether there was a threat implied, Jimmy clarified the situation. 'You get on home now, Mister, 'cos there is one of 'ee and three of we and one dawg.'

'Yes,' said the communard stoutly. He was one of the weediest of a weedy bunch. Elfrieda, the commander's wife, had once remarked on how slim the male communards were, particularly about the posterior. The commander put it down to permanent dysentery brought on by their revolting diet of beans and nettles.

The inspector looked at Patsy who was leaning on her elbows peering vaguely about her, at Jimmy, at the communard and at the commander. He raised his upper lip and puffed his moustache at them as a gesture of his contempt. It looked as if he had a large bloody butcher trout fly beneath his nose. 'Right! I shall make an official inspection of the premises tomorrow at 11am. And I'll make sure I have the police with me in case of any repetition of this ridiculous behaviour.' He dusted down his jacket as he retired to his car. 'And you, Sir!' He pointed a quivering forefinger at Jimmy. 'That dog of yours made an unprovoked attack. I shall lay a complaint and I intend to see that it is destroyed.'

'You'd better be jolly quick about it, otherwise Nature will beat you to it,' said the commander, looking down at Patsy who, still on her elbows, was mournfully contemplating the dozen long yards between her and the haven of the front doormat. The inspector started his car and accelerated away with Jimmy waving two gnarled fingers after him.

By eleven o'clock the following morning, everything was ready. It had been rushed, but a team of volunteers had been working on the house and the barn since shortly after dawn. They had glued moss on parts of the new roof ridge of the barn and the commander, with a stroke of genius, had plaited an extra dozen feet of ivy into the plant which already covered the gable end so that it embraced the ridge, making it look as if it had been there for decades.

The squire had put on his Guards tie, a sure sign that he was going to take his duties seriously. Percy was stamping his boots in the lane, chatting with Jason, while Keith and Frank finished the dismantling of the scaffolding, giving last critical looks at the barn. The squire went over to Jimmy who was in his front garden so that he would not miss any of the fun.

'Where is this damn fellow, eh, Jimmy?' he asked.

'I reckon we frightened him off yesterday. You should have seen my Patsy, Squire. She knocked him flying!' Jimmy looked fondly over to the doormat where Patsy was stretched out as usual.

'I hear that there may be a bit of trouble about that.'

'I hope so. The vet was on his way past to a calving at Ivor's a couple of days ago and I waved him down to take a look at her. He said she'd only got another few months before it would be right to put her down. £5, it'd cost me. £5 to kill my own dog!' Jimmy shook his head sadly, the smoke from his cigarette weaving a figure of eight in the still morning air as he did so.

'£5! Good Lord!' said the squire sympathetically.

'I've always shot my dogs before. It don't seem right to have to pay someone else to kill your own dog.'

'I know what you mean. My wife had a fall in 1971 on the first meet of the season. The animal broke its leg and she insisted on shooting it herself.'

'I remember that. That was a fine stag, killed just above the old weir, that day. I got its liver.'

'That's right.' The squire did not hunt but he respected the important place that the staghounds occupied in the local culture. His own pleasure lay in the slaughter of about 2,000 pheasants a year.

'I was hoping, Squire, you being a magistrate and all, that when Patsy goes to court, you might order her to be destroyed. That means she'll die a hero like, and I won't have to pay for it.'

The squire patted Jimmy reassuringly on the shoulder. 'A bit like a soldier dying for his country, eh? I'll see what I can do. If you get sent a summons, make sure you tell me the date and, even if I'm not on the bench, I'll leave word about it.'

There was the sound of a car engine coming down the lane. The squire turned to look. 'Ah!' he said rather nervously. 'This looks like the fellow now.'

The fellow was in his red car which drew up alongside Percy. The squire strode over to join them with his hands clasped behind his back, looking rather like Prince Philip.

'Good morning,' said the inspector, looking round at the welcoming party. 'I'm glad the law is present.'

'I'm not actually the law,' said the squire, 'although I am a magistrate.'

83

'Well, *you're* certainly the law, Constable. My name is Partridge. I'm the building inspector and I'd like to report that I was threatened by a man in his fifties with a bushy grey moustache yesterday. Right here.'

'I don't know anything about that,' replied Percy.

'That old man was a witness,' said the inspector, pointing to Jimmy. 'In fact he threatened me as well and his dog attacked me. I've already laid a complaint about it.'

'In that case it will be investigated in its due time,' replied Percy placidly. He was on familiar ground here as a goodly proportion of his official duties consisted of smoothing over feathers ruffled during clashes between opposing cultures – hunters *v.* saboteurs, farmers *v.* ramblers, villagers *v.* tourists. 'But I'm not here to talk about that, I'm here to ask a couple of questions about certain allegations concerning the corruption of public officials.'

Partridge cocked an inquiring eyebrow. 'Has that remark got anything to do with me?'

'I didn't say that, but if the hat fits . . .'

'Quite,' agreed the squire, nodding his head sagely.

The inspector examined the two of them carefully, assessing the nature of this attack. He had had some of his actions questioned in the past, but only by incomers who were trying to extend their newly bought cottages and did not understand the local customs. Country people knew all about the little perks of his job. Everyone either defrauded the Inland Revenue or the Social Security and it was in nobody's interest to demand too searching a scrutiny of the standard of integrity in their public officials.

'What exactly do you mean?'

'Well . . . er . . . you know.'

'No, I don't know.'

Percy sighed heavily. 'If you want me to spell it out, it was about that conversation you had with Frank over there.' He nodded his head towards Frank who was doing his best to keep out of the way during this stage of the business, just in case something went wrong.

The squire and Percy had a tiger by the tail. The inspector

84

smiled, a sight that made them both uneasy. 'You're Percy Chilcott, aren't you?'

'Constable Chilcott to you, Sir.'

'You've got a sister who lives out near Muddiford. I was passing there the other day and I saw that they've just put up a garage. Without planning permission.' He clicked his tongue. 'Awful pity if the authorities got to know of it. Don't you agree, Constable?'

Percy sighed a great sigh as he saw another rock being added to the cairn of compromise that is the human condition.

'Well, I haven't got a sister,' stated the squire. 'At least, not down here. I've got one up in Scotland. Married a Catholic. Lives in one of those icy castles with a positive farrow of children. Does it to keep warm, I suppose. The Eskimos do it in igloos a lot.'

'It's all right,' said the inspector kindly. 'As long as the constable has a sister, you don't need any relations at all.'

'Really? Is everything sorted out then?'

'Yes, Squire,' replied Percy. 'We know just where we stand now. You were a great help.'

'Oh good. Well, I might as well wander off now.' The squire wandered off, pleased that he had fulfilled familial obligations to his people once again. 'Everything's sorted out,' he told Jimmy happily as he walked past. 'Spot of fishing now, I think. The salmon are running, you know.'

'Good luck to you, Squire,' replied Jimmy, who had a twelve-pound fish, complete with pitchfork holes, simmering in a kettle on his pre-war Aga.

'Now we've got rid of him, let's take a look at this house,' said the inspector briskly. 'Judging by our little talk, it may be quite interesting.'

'I wouldn't know about that,' answered Percy. 'But I think I'd better be getting on with my duties now.'

'Oh no you don't. I demanded police protection, remember?'

Percy looked at him, his eyes those of the picture of Dorian Gray after an early trawl through Limehouse by its subject. 'I don't reckon you need any protecting, Sir. That silly red moustache of yours should give people plenty of warning to

85

leave you well alone. If you'll excuse me, Sir, I'll just go and have a word with Mr Mattock.' Percy touched the brim of his helmet and walked heavily over to Frank to impart the news that the inspector had not only not been nobbled, but was also fully alerted to the probability of skulduggery. Jimmy hobbled out from behind his wall to fill the hiatus left by the departure of the squire and Percy.

'Morning.'

'Oh, it's you. Morning,' replied the inspector, who had reached into the back window ledge of his car to collect his yellow safety helmet. 'No heart attacks today?'

'Where's Percy going?'

'I don't know, but he's got his tail between his legs. Where's that matelot friend of yours?'

'The commander? He's gone into town to sell some tomatoes.'

'That's a shame. I hoped he might be around to see this. I'm sure you'll make sure he hears about it, though.'

'Hears about what?'

'How I made your friend rip his damn house down. This bit is always exciting, listening to them squirm when they make excuses.'

Jimmy examined him as white corpuscle would a bacterium. 'You're a nasty sort of a fellow, aren't you?'

'Piss off, Grandad,' replied the inspector.

'Piss off yourself. Anyway, they've done what you told them to.'

'What?' The inspector turned for the first time to look at the roof ridges. His jaw dropped. 'Jesus! I don't believe it! How on earth did they manage that?'

'Aha!' crowed Jimmy. 'That surprised you, didn't it? It doesn't matter how they did it, just so long as it's done. Now you have to give it your approval.'

'I don't understand. There's got to be something going on otherwise what was all that business about yesterday? And why was that daft policeman coming the heavy with me?'

Frank, seeing the inspector looking at the roof, decided that it was time he went over to hear the worst. 'Good morning,

Mr Partridge,' he said glumly.

Partridge turned a bewildered face towards Frank. 'The roof. How did you do it?'

Frank interpreted bewilderment as the expected accusation and decided to come clean. 'Corrugated iron', he replied briefly. 'I'm sorry that—' The rest of what he was about to reveal was drowned out by Jimmy who deemed that the moment was right to do his duty once more. 'Aah!' he yelled, clutching at his heart.

'Oh not again!' complained Partridge, stepping swiftly backwards a few paces. 'What do you mean, "corrugated iron"? How can you reduce the height of a building with corrugated iron?'

Frank heard but failed to understand the import of the inspector's remark as he was transfixed by Jimmy's performance. Unlike the inspector, he had not seen it before. Jimmy stopped clutching his chest but his face was suddenly contorted in an enormous, agonized grimace. It was only when the spasm was repeated, even more violently than before, that Frank realized that Jimmy was winking and then managed to work out why. He felt a tiny spark glow amid the damp kindling of his hopes.

'Corrugated iron! Ah! Yes! Nice morning, isn't it? Very good of you to come. See? We managed to lower the building all right.'

'You won't get away with it. You must have reduced the ceiling height upstairs and that'll make them lower than you're allowed.'

'We didn't lower the ceilings.'

'Well, what did you do then?'

'Don't you go telling him,' interrupted Jimmy. 'He's just here to make sure you abide by his silly rules. You don't have to tell him your trade secrets.'

'Don't worry,' Frank reassured him. 'If you can't find out for yourself, Mr Partridge, I'm certainly not going to tell you.'

'So you're still not prepared to co-operate? Right, we'll just have to have a look. I've been doing this job for twenty years. You won't be able to keep any secrets from me!' The optimism in the inspector's voice had taken on a note of defiance which was not lost on his audience. Feeling more cheerful by the second, Frank led the inspector to the house to join Keith and Jason and they all went in.

'Ha!' cried Partridge, unable to conceal his disappointment. 'You haven't lowered these ceilings.'

'That's right,' agreed Keith. 'We haven't had to make any changes here.'

'Let's go upstairs, then.' Partridge almost trotted through the hall to the stairs, taking them two at a time.

'If you were doing your job right, you'd be taking a proper look around down here,' shouted Jason reprovingly at his ascending backside.

'There's no point,' it replied, 'if the whole place is coming down.' Keith and Jason climbed after him. He had his steel rule out and was running it up the bedroom wall. He checked it and checked again. 'The roof!' he cried, feverishly. 'You must have reduced the height of this roof. We specified the pitch. You aren't allowed to alter it.'

'The trapdoor is in the bathroom,' said Keith equably.

'But I'll need a stepladder. It's no good not providing me with a ladder. You have to give me every assistance on my inspection. I'd just be back with a court order and a sensible policeman.'

Keith was enjoying himself. He, like Frank, doubted if they would get away with this stratagem but there were compensations whatever the outcome. 'We've got a stepladder in the bathroom all ready for you.'

'Oh! You have, have you?' The inspector squared his shoulders. 'We'll soon see about that.'

'Exactly,' said Jason.

Partridge suspiciously examined the ladder to ensure that it was not booby-trapped. He grasped it firmly in both hands, shook it as if it were a thicket of jungle bamboo and climbed resolutely upwards. He paused at the top to raise an enquiring eyebrow at Keith, who pointedly retreated outside the bathroom door to flick a switch which flooded the loft space with 500 watts of illumination. There was foreboding in

Partridge's face as he finally disappeared through the bathroom ceiling.

'E.T. going home,' croaked Jason, sitting on the avocado-green lavatory. Keith gave a comfortable chuckle and they waited placidly for a minute or two until a shadow over the trapdoor announced the re-appearance of Partridge. 'All right,' he hissed, his spittle being atomized through the fine sieve of his moustache to drift down the beam of light into the bath. 'I give up. How did you manage it?'

'We lowered it,' replied Keith, speaking softly since he was witnessing one whose cup of triumph had been cruelly dashed from his lips.

'Lowered it! I can see you bloody lowered it. But how? This roof slope is exactly as specified.'

'Of course it is. We're craftsmen, not cowboys.'

'But you must have had it too steep before!'

'Perhaps we did and perhaps we didn't.'

'It would have cost a fortune to take it down and replace it!'

'If it did, it's not your problem, is it?'

'I'm coming down.' He descended, turning to peer into Keith's face when he reached the bottom. 'That's it, isn't it? It cost a fortune, didn't it? You had to work day and night, didn't you? And all that business with the scaffolding and that old man and the policeman was just to wind me up, wasn't it?'

'If that's the way it was, it's none of your business, is it?' remarked Keith.

'Exactly,' agreed Jason, receiving an approving nod from Keith for using the word in its correct context for once.

'I won, then, didn't I?'

'I didn't know we were in a competition,' replied Keith. 'Is the inspection over, then?'

'Not till I see Frank Mattock.' Partridge pushed past and clumped down the stairs, darting suspicious glances to his right and left. There was small comfort for him. Keith may have been a little shaky when it came to the big picture, but detailed finishing was his speciality. He could hang a hundred horse brasses along a wall at precisely six-inch intervals by eye alone.

Outside Frank was pacing up and down nervously, worried that either Keith or Jason might lose their nerve and babble out their guilt. Jimmy had tried to pace as well, but had given up and was now resting his backside on the bonnet of the red car.

When the inspector appeared in the doorway, Frank tried to muster a confident smile, but managed only to look shifty. The inspector came over to him. 'I'm sorry it had to be this way, Mr Mattock.'

'What way?' asked Frank guardedly.

'That you had to spend so much extra money on lowering your roof, of course.' The inspector sensed that he had missed something, but he could not identify what it was. 'What else did you think I meant?'

'Ah, yes! That way! Yes, it has really taught me a lesson. Next time I do some work, I'll know who to get to draw up plans. You can rest assured on that. I've certainly learned my lesson. Oh yes. I've learned my lesson all right.' Frank put an unconvincing arm round Partridge's shoulder and steered him towards the car.

Partridge stopped. 'You're not angry! None of you are angry with me! That's what's wrong! Why aren't you angry?'

'You're only doing your job' – Frank suddenly saw quicksands – 'you bastard!'

'You're up to something. You should be yelling at me, not being so damn reasonable. I've just cost you thousands of pounds. There's something funny going on here. That copper was trying to put the squeeze on me and he sure as hell wasn't very practised at it. He must have had a good reason.'

'No, no, none at all,' protested Frank.

It was unfortunate that the inspector had been a few minutes late for his appointment. If he had been on time, he would have been gone by the time the church clock suddenly hammered the tenor bell in the tower to signal the half-hour. Its vibrations gave this year's rooks the excuse for which they were waiting to leap from their perches on the top of the clump of beeches at the end of the churchyard and wheel, cawing, into the sky under the indulgent eye of their parents.

'You're pulling a fast one, somehow. I don't know what it is, but it's something,' continued the inspector.

Frank began to burble. 'It's nothing,' he said. 'Really, truly, it's nothing. I couldn't pull something on you, now, could I? You're Mr Partridge, isn't he, Jimmy? You're a right hard-nosed bastard. You've cost me a fortune. I hate you, I really do, don't I, Jimmy? Jimmy?'

Jimmy was not paying attention. It was just as well that Partridge was, because there was an expression of horrified dismay on the old man's face. Frank turned his head to follow the line of his gaze. It ended on a trio of the young rooks. They had had enough of wheeling and had come to roost on the roof ridge of the barn and, to their raucous surprise, the commander's plaited ivy had unplaited. A green curtain swished away from the roof to leave, gapingly visible, the naked gap between the original line of the roof and its addition.

'Urrggh!' remarked Jimmy.

Frank could not help but agree: 'Urrggh!'

'What?' asked Partridge, who still had his back to the incident.

'Urrggh!' Jimmy repeated and rather wearily clutched at his chest.

'Oh no, please, not again,' begged Partridge. 'This is getting boring.'

Jimmy was afraid of that, but he had an extra prop to add to the efficacy of his distraction display. 'Urrggh!' he cried again, rolled his eyeballs, and began to drum his heels on the paintwork of the car against which he was resting.

'Watch it, you old fool! Mind my car!' Partridge sprang forward and jerked Jimmy off his perch. Jimmy staggered forward but he knew, if he showed sufficient purpose, that he could win the day with his heroism and put Frank many pints in his debt. He grimly came back in, his army surplus boots poised to thud into the door of the car. 'What the hell do you think you're doing? That car's council property! Stop it!'

'Get your vehicle out of here!' shouted Frank, sizing up the situation. 'When he gets like this, he can't help what he's doing.' Frank put his arms round Jimmy, pinioning him loosely, and supported him towards the back of the car – away from the barn. Partridge hesitated, so Jimmy squinted through a half-closed eyelid and made contact with a rear light. The crack of splitting plastic was the clincher. The inspector scuttled round to the driving seat of his car and jumped in.

'Don't forget to send me a certificate,' shouted Frank happily. 'You might as well send me a bill for your light as well. You're too smart for us. We tried to pretend that it was easy to lower the roof, but we couldn't fool you.'

Partridge afforded himself one final poisoned look at Frank before he put his car in gear and disappeared down the lane, drawing seed parachutes from the willowherb that swayed in the hedgerow at his passage.

Jason walked over to Jimmy. 'You wicked old devil!' he said admiringly. 'I wouldn't have believed it if I hadn't seen it!' As Jimmy blushed beneath his dirt and wrinkles, Jason leaned forward and gave him a smacking kiss on his cheek.

'You disgusting young bastard!' Jimmy clapped one hand to his cheek as though it had been branded and swiped with the stick in the other at Jason, who skipped away with the fluid ease of youth. Jimmy turned to Frank: 'That's got to be worth at least six months of tick in the pub, Frank.'

'How much do you drink?' asked Frank.

'I never have more than one pint of beer an evening, do I, Jason?'

'Never more than one pint,' grinned Jason.

'All right. I'll tell Helga that the next six months of your drinks are on me – as long as you promise that you'll have no more than one pint of beer a night.'

'Thanks.'

'Well done, you two,' Frank continued. 'It's been a great day for the village.'

'And your pocket,' said Jason.

'Well, I'm not complaining. I'd better get back to the farm. I've got a hundred heifers to dose.' Frank walked contentedly over to his car, parked near the lychgate.

'Would you two like a cup of tea after all that excitement?' asked Jimmy.

'Thanks', said Keith.

'No more than one pint, you old bugger! I've seen you knock back a bottle of whisky when you've had money in your pocket.'

'He said he'd pay as long as I didn't drink more than one pint of beer a night. He didn't say anything about scotch.'

'He didn't say anything about you not buying me beer, either.'

'Nor'e did. He'll pay for his bloody roof yet, or I'm not the Jimmy I think I am!'

And he did.

Chapter Seven

'THE RUSTLE of money.'

'The baying of a pack of hounds in the distance.'

'The whistle of a bosun's pipe when you go on board your first command.'

'The rush of beer from a hand pump.'

'The squeal of a rabbit when a ferret grabs hold of her.'

The topic for discussion at the WI meeting that evening had been 'The Most Beautiful Sound in the World'. The crackle of a log fire had been the winner among the ladies, but the men in the pub showed a wider choice.

'Yuk! I don't like yours, Gerald,' said the commander. 'That's horrid!'

'You can't have heard it,' replied Gerald, his pint tankard almost hidden in his huge hands. Gerald was a farmer in his forties who wrested a living from the edge of the moor by brute force, of which he had a large amount. The consuming passion of both himself and his wife, Mary, was field sports. 'It makes the hair on the back of your neck prickle. I like my shooting and I like my hunting, but ferreting's what I like best of all. It's so sort of intimate.'

'I can't imagine what the fun of it is,' replied the commander with a shudder.

'Haven't you ever been ferreting?' asked Gerald.

'No.'

Kelvin tut-tutted. 'Surely you must have done when you were a nipper? Everybody goes ferreting when they're kids.'

'Not in Eastbourne, we didn't.

'Well, you missed something. In the old days, ferrets were

94

proper ferrets. People really bothered about them and made them really tame. They're wild as hawks these days.'

'I've got a ferret at the moment that's the best animal I've ever seen. Bloody amazing animal it is. Shove it down a hole and the rabbits pop out like rats from a burning rick,' announced Gerald smugly.

'Fat chance,' said Kelvin with scorn. 'I haven't handled the beasts for twenty years but the old skills have died out. I had a ferret that would sip milk from my tongue.'

'Good grief!' exclaimed the commander. 'What a bizarre picture! Why on earth would you want it to do that?'

'It shows how tame it is.'

Gerald shifted his large buttocks on the stool. He hid his muscle under a layer of protective blubber which spilled over the belt of his trousers and bulged, hairily, through the buttonless gaps in his cotton shirt. 'You and the commander ought to come out and see her in action some time.'

'How about tomorrow morning?' asked Kelvin. Prudence had strained her back shifting ten tonnes of fertilizer. With her *hors de combat*, there was nobody to do Kelvin's work for him so he could take time off. 'You can come, can't you, Commander?'

'I don't think I can. I've got to do some weeding.'

'Don't be silly. The weeds'll still be there tomorrow but the chance of a bit of ferreting won't be. We'll both come, Gerald.'

'I don't know that I can manage tomorrow. I've got 300 sheep to sort out.'

'I've got a warren in one of my hedges that's like the ones you used to get before the myxomatosis. I was going to get Jimmy to help me gas it, but if you could come out tomorrow . . . ' Kelvin was one of nature's Machiavellians, but this was child's play as he knew he was on to a racing certainty.

'Really?' queried Gerald eagerly. 'I couldn't miss a chance like that. What sort of time?'

'About half ten. OK, Commander?'

'I don't see why not. It's all experience, isn't it?'

The commander liaised with Kelvin at the top of his farm lane in the lay-by which allowed the milk lorry to pull in to empty

Kelvin's tank without blocking the road. They both had their shotguns. Gerald's Land Rover was soon audible and visible above the hedgerows since it was without a silencer and trailed a blizzard of straw, twine and empty paper sacks that had once contained half-hundredweights of cattle nuts. They watched in silence as it rattled round the corner, sheepdogs peering over and round the cab from the back, and pulled in behind the commander's Subaru. Gerald got out, clutching a green felt bag, and snarled at the dogs who hung their panting heads over the tailgate of the vehicle.

'You've got a real treat coming, Kelvin,' he announced.

'Let's have a squint at the bugger, then.'

'Hang on,' said Gerald, swinging the bag gently away from Kelvin's grasping hand. 'You'll frighten her. She doesn't know you. I'll open it for you.' He delicately loosed the drawstring and peered slowly inside, making a kissing sound with his lips. He held the bag out to Kelvin who peered inside.

'Huh! It doesn't look much. Damn thing looks a bit dopey to me. Are you sure it's not been overfed?'

Gerald snatched the bag away. 'Overfed?' he snapped. 'It's in fighting condition, you ignorant old bugger. Just let me point her to a rabbit hole.'

Kelvin hefted his gun to his shoulder. 'Well, what are we hanging about for? We'll soon see.' He led the way to the opposite side of the road and through a muddy gateway into a field that looked as if it had been made over to the cultivation of rushes and thistles. They squelched a couple of hundred yards across to a hedgerow that separated the field from a tangled beech wood.

Gerald examined it in silence. 'There are a few holes here, I suppose.'

'What do you mean, "a few holes"?' said Kelvin indignantly. 'It's not a hedge any more. It's one of them Tom and Jerry cheeses.'

Gerald delved into a poacher's pocket inside his green jacket and pulled out a handful of nets. 'Let's get on with it, then. You block up holes this side and I'll go the other.'

The commander hunched his shoulders against a biting

wind that scudded the clouds above the trees. He watched Gerald carefully negotiate the gap between a couple of healthy young oaks that were sprouting in the unkempt hedgerow while Kelvin crabbed across the base of the bank in front of him, carefully tying nets over fifteen yards of holes. 'What did we bring the guns along for, Kelvin?'

'To shoot rabbits with, you fool!'

'But aren't they supposed to get stuck in the nets?'

'It's a smart rabbit that'll get through a net that I've laid out, but it's possible. A big old buck can be travelling when it hits the net and some will go round the ends.' He straightened his back with a groan. 'No wonder I gave up this game years ago. Still, it's nice to watch a good animal work and it's exciting waiting for the rabbits to come out.'

There was a yell from the other side of the hedge. 'Are you ready, Kelvin?'

'Yes!' called back Kelvin. 'Commander, you stand one side of the nets and I'll stand at the other, and for Christ's sake, wait till the rabbit is out in the field before you shoot it. They can come out damn fast and I don't want you waving your gun at me.'

The commander, as well as being cold, was now rather nettled. 'Kelvin, I may not take my gun to bed with me, but I know what I'm doing.'

'Good.' Kelvin raised his voice: 'Get on with it, then, Gerald!'

'She's just going in now!' yelled Gerald. 'Go on, my beauty. Get down there. Go on!'

Kelvin thumbed back the hammers on his gun with a double click that had chilled the hearts of generations of small furry and feathery creatures on the farm ever since his grandfather had bought the weapon, second-hand, to mark the coronation of Edward VII. 'This is the bit I like,' he said with a grin. 'It's so bloody exciting, isn't it?'

'Yes, I suppose it is,' agreed the commander with an answering smile. He was disarmed to hear Kelvin actually admit to a spontaneous emotion. 'You never know what or when.'

A rabbit erupted from its burrow behind Kelvin. His gun
leapt to his shoulder and discharged, to the detriment of a
clump of rushes about eight feet in front of him. He swore,
pulled the trigger again and there was a click. 'Bloody
cardboard cartridges!' he roared. 'They get damp in them if
you keep them for a year or two. Why can't they make them
out of plastic like everything else?'

The commander laughed. 'When did you last buy any?
They've been plastic for years.'

Kelvin paused in the act of reloading his gun to deliver a
crushing retort, but none came into his mind. A rabbit nipped
out of the hedgerow and scampered past him. The commander
chuckled. Kelvin glared at him. 'It would be more use if you
shot the blasted animals rather than just sniggering at
them.'

'They're not coming out my side.'

'Behind you!' shouted Kelvin.

The commander swung round, the barrel of his shotgun
hunting for a target. A rabbit had emerged from a burrow. It

gave one horrified glance and dived back underground before the trigger was pulled. The commander smoothly adjusted his aim and blew another to a better world. 'I got one, Kelvin!'

'Big deal!' came the scornful reply. 'It's like shooting ducks in a barrel.'

'How many ducks have you shot?' asked the commander.

'And I thought I told you to wait until the brutes were out into the field before you fired. That last one was not even out of its burrow. If you can't be a safe shot, you've no right to be out.'

'That was perfectly safe shooting and, anyway, you yelled "Behind you", ' responded the commander in annoyance. Another rabbit emerged from under Kelvin's feet. His thumb slipped on the hammers of his gun as he pulled them back to cock and the left barrel exploded, punching a tight pattern of shot through the hedge. '—Which is more than can be said for that!'

'That was an accident,' replied Kelvin defensively, raising his voice above a roar of rage from Gerald.

'You amaze me! I thought you were trying to shoot him deliberately,' said the commander.

There was silence for a couple of minutes with both hunters remaining tense, waiting for more prey to present itself. Kelvin shifted his feet, the mud squelching beneath his wellingtons. 'There are a damn sight more rabbits down there than we've seen so far. That ferret isn't doing its job.'

'If there are that many of them, perhaps they've ganged up against the beast and beaten it up or something.'

'Don't be stupid.'

There was another damp silence. The trees of the wood overhung the field and the wind shook chill teardrops from the leaves down the back of the commander's neck. 'How long do we have to wait?'

'I dunno,' responded Kelvin. 'If there aren't any more rabbits there, Gerald should try the ferret somewhere else. I'll give him a shout.' Kelvin walked over to the hedge. 'Gerald! There's bugger all going on over here. Bring up your ferret and let's try further along.'

Gerald's face reared into view through the lattice-work of brambles. 'There's bugger all going on over here as well. The ferret's down there somewhere, but I don't reckon there are many coneys around.'

'Pull her out and let's try a bit further along.'

'OK. Did you get many?'

'One or two,' replied Kelvin, airily.

'Huh!' grunted Gerald. 'Apart from the one aimed at me, there were at least another three shots.'

'True, but the rabbits were bolting fifty yards up the hedge. There are none in the nets which there should have been if your ferret was doing her job.'

'I've been offered £250 for that animal.'

'It just proves there are plenty of idiots around.'

The commander shivered and stamped his feet. 'Can we get on with it? I'm cold.'

Kelvin turned from the hedge and broke his gun, laying it on the wet grass. 'We'll get these nets in, Gerald.' He and the commander unpegged the nets from the front of the burrows and piled them by Kelvin's gun. 'Where's your rabbit?'

'Er . . . actually it fell back down its burrow. I fired a bit too soon.'

'Well go and get it, then,' ordered Kelvin scornfully.

'I had a look when I got the nets and I'm afraid I couldn't tell which burrow was which.'

'It's just as well you've got someone to wipe your arse for you,' said Kelvin. 'I marked the hole when I saw it put its head out. If I pick it up, can I have it?'

'Feel free. But let's get on with it. Standing around in a cold wet field is not my idea of a fun afternoon.'

Kelvin walked up the hedgerow, a sneer on his face as he considered the barrenness of spirit of someone who could casually give away a rabbit he had just shot. He walked to the burrow, pushed his arm inside it and pulled out the corpse. He held it above his head, brandishing it at the commander. 'Ha!' he yelled. 'There's a damn good dinner there!' Although the commander was twenty-five yards away Kelvin could sense that there was something amiss. It may have been the

100

fact that he nearly dropped his gun or the high-pitched whimper that escaped between his lips. 'What's wrong?'

The commander shot a furtive glance at the hedge and back at Kelvin. 'The rabbit!' he called hoarsely, walking swiftly across.

'What?' Kelvin looked for the first time at the animal which dangled, slackly, by his side. 'Jesus!' he whispered. 'It's not a rabbit.'

'I didn't think it was,' said the commander miserably.

'It's a fucking ferret. It's Gerald's fucking ferret.' It was Kelvin's turn to look fearfully at the hedge. 'What the hell did you go and shoot it for?'

'I didn't do it deliberately, for Christ's sake! I thought it was a rabbit. You did too. You yelled at me to shoot it. What are we going to do?'

Kelvin dropped the ferret and backed away from it. 'It's nothing to do with me, mate. You shot the bloody thing.'

'You told me to,' hissed the commander. 'We're in this together.'

'We're bloody not. Gerald'll tear your head off. He's not

having mine off too. Take my advice. Own up and get it over with.'

'I'll go one better than take your advice. I'll do what you would do under the circumstances.'

Kelvin fingered his gun nervously. 'What's that?'

'I'll tell him it was you that shot it.'

Kelvin grimaced in horror. 'You wouldn't! I'd tell him the truth!'

'Which one of us do you think he'd believe?'

'You bastard!'

'Here!' came a voice from down the hedge. 'Have you seen my Betty?'

Kelvin turned to the commander. 'Hide the damn thing! Quick!' The commander nipped smartly across to the hedge and deposited the departed wonderbeast back down its rabbit hole.

'Have you seen my Betty?' repeated Gerald.

The commander emitted a squeak of alarm as there was now only the thickness of the hedge between them. 'Betty? Betty? Who's Betty?' he asked wildly.

'The ferret, of course. If there were no rabbits left down there, she should have been out by now. What's wrong? You sound a bit funny.'

'Nothing's wrong. No, I haven't seen your Betty.'

Gerald appeared on top of the hedgebank. 'It's not like her, you know. She's never stayed down like this before. I can't understand it.'

'You should have put a bell round her neck,' said Kelvin. 'She'll be down there eating a rabbit and she won't be coming out until she's finished.'

'But I fed her just before we came out!'

'Have you brought a spade to dig her out?'

'No. I tell you, she never stays down.'

'She'll be out and into the wood then. She'll be long gone. You'll never find her. We might as well go home.'

'She's still down there. There aren't that many holes the other side and those that I didn't net I stopped up.' Gerald looked broodingly down at the commander. 'Give me a rabbit and I'll paunch it and try to lure her out.'

'A rabbit! Yes, a rabbit. That's a good idea. Kelvin, he wants a rabbit.'

'Well he can't bloody well have one. We didn't get any.'

'No! That's it! We didn't get any!'

Gerald looked puzzled. 'I thought you said you'd got a few, Kelvin. What were you shooting at apart from me?'

'It was the commander and he kept missing.'

Gerald sighed. 'What a bloody shambles! Stick your head down a hole and see if you can hear her.'

Kelvin did as he was requested. The brambles prevented Gerald from climbing down from the hedgebank to join him but he watched as Kelvin prostrated himself before Betty's burial chamber with his gun by his side, for all the world like an elderly Druze militiaman when the muezzin presses 'Play' and the speakers blare from the Beirut minarets. 'I can't hear anything,' said Kelvin after a few seconds.

'I'll go and listen my side.' Gerald disappeared.

Kelvin peered over his shoulder. 'Has he gone?' The commander nodded. Kelvin rose to his feet. 'Even if there had been any underground noises, I wouldn't have heard them through that ferret. I think you'd better get it out of there. He'll be down this burrow himself before he gives up on it.'

The commander put his arm down the hole and retrieved the muddy, bedraggled fleshy envelope of Betty. He trotted 150 yards down the hedge and stuffed it down another hole. He was flushed and panting by the time he returned to see Kelvin climbing one way through the hedge and Gerald coming the other. 'Right, Commander. I'm going off to get a spade. Kelvin's going to watch the other side of the hedge and you watch this.'

'How long will you be?'

'Not more than twenty minutes.'

The commander lifted his arm in a half-hearted farewell as Gerald hurried off up the field. 'Kelvin, this has all the hallmarks of becoming ridiculous.'

'Has he gone?'

'Yes.'

103

Kelvin heaved himself back over the hedge. 'It is bloody ridiculous. But it won't be if he digs it up.'

'Can't we produce the remains when he gets back and say that it tripped when it came out of a hole and broke its neck, or something?'

'Not when it's half its head missing. It couldn't have landed with a thump like that off those little legs.'

'Let's say someone else came along and shot it.'

'Why? Who was it? And what were we doing at the time?'

'Well, you suggest something, then.'

'I would suggest that we keep bullshitting if we want to keep healthy. He loved that bloody animal.'

The sound of the Land Rover's return gave Kelvin plenty of warning of scramble back over the hedge and take up watch and they both continued to evince concern as the spade made several abortive forays into the underworld during the following hour. After that they just stood around and waited for a while. It was 1.30 before they found themselves back in the pub, putting chattering whiskies to their mouths.

'What have you three been up to?' inquired Jason Loosemire.

'Ferreting,' replied Kelvin shortly.

'Any luck?'

'No. It got lost.'

'It's my best ferret,' said Gerald. 'It's terrible.'

'Not Betty?' asked Jason in shocked tones.

'Yes.'

'What a shame! I lost my Horace last week. Where did you lose Betty?'

'That hedge by Gliddon's Wood.'

'That's where I lost mine!'

'What!' shouted Kelvin. 'How dare you go down there without permission!'

'The wood belongs to the squire,' protested Jason. 'It's got more rabbits than anywhere else.'

'But this side of the hedge is mine.'

'I no more went your side of the hedge than you went the squire's side this morning.'

'The bare-faced cheek of it! Do you hear? He's admitting he's been poaching. I'll set Percy on you, Jason!' threatened Kelvin.

'Psst!' said the commander.

'What is it?' asked Gerald.

'No, not you. I was wanting a quiet word with Kelvin.'

'Me? What is it?'

The commander raised his eyebrows in exasperation. 'I said a *quiet* word.'

'Can't it wait?'

'No, it bloody can't! For heaven's sake!' The commander dragged Kelvin away from the bar and towards the fire. 'That ferret of Jason's. It could have been that one that I shot and not Betty at all. I thought it a bit funny that the thing came out so quickly. If it was Jason's, it could have been lonely and come out when it heard our voices.'

'So what?'

'Don't you see? Betty could still be there.'

'So what?'

'We could go back there and she could easily be there waiting for us.'

'Do you want to go back there? Back to the wet and cold? All for some vicious little rodent?'

'Is a ferret a rodent?'

''Tain't a cow or a fox, so it must be a rodent.'

'No.'

'Yes, it is.'

'I meant I don't want to go back to the cold and the wet.'

'Then keep your mouth shut.'

'Have you sorted everything out, then?' asked Gerald as they returned to the bar.

'Yes, replied Kelvin. He drained his glass.

'In that case let's get back there and see if Betty has come out yet.' Both the commander and Kelvin groaned. Gerald's eyes narrowed. 'You both care about Betty, don't you?'

'Oh yes, we cared,' said the commander, having watched the way the sod had flown from Gerald's spade and the

105

muscles on his back had rippled his heavy oiled-cotton jacket. 'We cared . . . er . . . care very much.'

'I should hope so. No sportsman would leave matters as they are.'

'Quite,' said the commander almost immediately.

'Let's go, then.'

'My leg,' said Kelvin, clutching his leg. 'It's my knee. Jason, you can take my place.'

'All right. I might find my Horace.'

'Let's go, then,' said Gerald.

The commander could have saved his poisonous look, for Kelvin did not even turn to say goodbye as he was busy getting in another drink before closing time.

The rain had passed over by the time they returned to the hedgerow, although the wind still howled mournfully through the honeycomb of tunnels and craters left by rabbit and shovel. There was no sign of life for the first half an hour. Then there was. 'There she is!' shouted Gerald. 'Up the hedge about 150 yards.' The hair on the back of the commander's neck prickled as he followed the outstretched arm to see a ferret emerge from the burial burrow. 'Quick! Before she goes down again.' The commander held back, fearful of what manifestation of the supernatural should be found and how much of it would be obviously missing due to shotgun wounds. 'Aah!' Gerald's hoarse cry as they approached skidded the commander to a halt. He watched cautiously. 'She's dead! My Betty's dead! That bastard must have killed her!' The commander began to edge quietly backwards. Gerald turned, his face working with emotion. 'Commander, come here!'

'No, look. I'm sorry, Gerald. It was an accident,' babbled the commander.

'An accident! Nonsense! It's bloody murder!' Gerald loomed before the commander, grabbed him by the collar of his jacket and dragged him over. The commander felt as if he'd been hooked by the jib of a crane. He struggled, but unavailingly. 'Look!'

He looked. A cry burst from his lips. There was Betty, or

106

most of Betty. Standing over her was another ferret chewing at a sinewy bit of her thigh. It looked up and peered at the witnesses with an expression of benign goodwill on its face.

'That's my Horace!' cried Jason.

'Kill the bastard!' shouted Gerald viciously.

'It's not Horace's fault,' said Jason, picking his animal up and thrusting it inside his jacket, leaving smears of blood on his shirt front.

'Kill it! Ferrets will fight and can kill each other, but look at Betty!' A great shuddering sigh of sadness shook his huge frame. He swallowed, shaking his head. "It's not right that she was torn to pieces. That's not natural. A ferret that can do that to its own kind is a bloody menace. You want to get rid of it before it attacks again. It could be a baby next time.'

'I suppose you're right,' said Jason sadly, feeling inside his shirt.

'Hang on a minute,' said the commander. 'I think we may be in danger of over-reacting here. It's not likely to come across many babies down a rabbit hole, after all. And we don't know for sure that it killed Betty.'

Gerald picked up the corpse and held it in his hand. 'You stick to what you know, Commander. That brute killed Betty all right. You can see the bite wound on the back of her neck.'

'But Betty may have been dead already and Jason's ferret may have just stumbled across her body.'

'Commander, you'll never make a decent countryman. You're too soft. Ferrets don't just die. Something or somebody has to kill them and that Horace was caught in the act. It's a shame, but there it is.' Gerald swung his arm and Betty sailed far above the hedge, above the trees, and came to her final rest deep in the wood.

Jason took out Horace and held it in front of his face. 'You never were much of a ferret, were you?'

'No!' said the commander. 'Don't do it!'

Gerald sighed again. 'We've no choice. A ferret that kills like that can't be used again.'

'Well don't use it again. Keep it as a pet or something, but don't kill it. You can't kill it just like that. There's a reasonable doubt about its guilt.'

'There isn't unless you know something that we don't know. I'll tell you what. If you want it to live so badly, Jason can give it to you. As long as you keep it by itself in a cage, it can't do any more damage. That'd be all right by you, Jason?'

'Sure,' replied Jason with a shrug. 'The commander can have it if he wants it.'

And the commander got it. It escaped from its orange box that night and disappeared, but not before killing ten of Elfrieda's chickens. Kelvin was the only person who found it funny.

Chapter Eight

AUTUMN IS the end of the agricultural year. Nature has done with her growing and creatures from squirrels to farmers check their stores of nuts, hay or silage to ensure that they have enough for the hungry months ahead. Full barns did not mean prosperity for just the farmers and squirrels, however. With a bit of luck they could lead to a bit of extra income for some of the young male villagers as well – up to £5 an hour, double the going rate for working in the garage, the cafe, on the farms or vaguely piling bricks on top of each other as they added desultory extensions to the houses of the village.

The source of this prosperity was one of the foundations of the community's civic pride. It had its own fire station, the only one for miles. Other villages may have been larger. Some may have been sufficiently pretentious to change the name of their elected rulers from parish councillors to town councillors. There was even one nearby hamlet which not only had fifteen street lights to the village's two, but had gone so far as to paint yellow lines along the edge of some of its streets to pretend to visitors that it could afford to pay traffic wardens; but this hamlet had no fire station

It was a source of great status to be or to have been a fireman. It was great fun too. There was enormous pleasure to be had from thundering round the countryside, lights flashing and klaxon blaring, a delightful surge of adrenalin coursing through the veins, wondering what excitements were to come. And there was also the money. The firemen had a network of informants, often girlfriends, who reported the faintest trace of smoke. The firemen had bleepers nowadays, but everyone looked back with nostalgia on the days of the old siren whose wail had echoed round the valley, wheeling the rooks like Junkers 88s above the cottages and fields, to summon the crew and alert the whole community to the drama.

The fire engine waited until the first half-dozen of the men sprinting through the village or roaring down the lanes in tatty vans, with doors flapping and seatbelts flying, had jumped, properly uniformed, on board; then it was off, tyres screeching, siren braying, scattering ducks and tourists while the crew stared straight ahead with steely jaws and grim purpose on their faces which broke only to jeer at their tardier colleagues whom they passed on their way through the village.

Mick, who ran the village cafe with his wife, was the fire chief and he ensured that his lads were kept well in training and had plenty of work to do. He made it clear to the community that he expected the brigade to be called out at the

110

least threat of a chimney fire or the smoulder of an electrical socket and everyone co-operated as best they could, although his penchant for blasting unattended bonfires with high-powered hoses caused some ill feeling, particularly since blackened, half-burnt debris could be sent hurtling into neighbouring gardens or smeared over pink-painted cottage walls. However, everyone knew it was important that the crew should be able to produce figures to prove that infernos were as frequent in the area as summer showers: this source of excitement and revenue for the community had to be justified.

It all remained rather unreal because nobody ever got hurt. In the 150-year period during which there had been known to be a specialized fire-fighting force of some description in the village, no fire had ever damaged any human being. The odd animal was roasted before its time and once the fire engine had crashed on its return journey resulting in a couple of broken limbs, but that was a natural hazard of return journeys. After a fire of any reasonable quality, it was only right that the nearest pub should be visited for a post mortem and a chance to water dry throats, so progress back to base was always rather erratic.

Spring and summer provided most of the bread-and-butter work for the brigade, but it was autumn that produced the jam. Autumn was the barn fire season. In the old days of a couple of decades ago, the countryside was pimpled by ricks, delightful constructions that burst into flames with enthusiasm when they were damp or when they received visits from the old-fashioned village idiots for whom arson was the normal mode of self-expression. It was one of the tragedies of progress that, just at the time when the brigade finally gained the mobility of a modern appliance, both the village idiot and the rick went out of fashion. The idiots became the handicapped and people looked after them, while hay and straw was baled up and stored under cover.

Progress could not alter the Laws of Nature, however. If hay was stored before it had dried out properly, it still heated up and could still catch fire. One needed to be a pretty lousy farmer to allow this to happen, but there was no shortage of

111

lousy farmers in the neighbourhood which led to plenty of work for the firemen. In the autumn, headquarters would be shuffling round their fire crews like Fighter Command during the Battle of Britain, moving fire engines halfway across the county to meet emergencies as they occurred. There was just such a crisis in progress the afternoon a barn went up only a few hundred yards from the pub.

The village machine was already out attending a flashy insubstantial affair that was roman-candling inside a patch of gorse, the sort of fire for which it is hardly worth unrolling the hoses, except that this one had been reported by the house-holder nearest to the blaze who was known to be the widowed mother of the assistant under-secretary of state at the Home Office with responsibility for the fire service.

Back in the unprotected village, the pub telephone rang towards the end of the midday session – although it did not so much ring as chirrup in the approved modern manner. Helga behind the bar picked it up, listened to it for a second and held the receiver out to Kelvin. He peered suspiciously at it before taking hold. It not only chirruped but also looked as if it would snap if grasped carelessly in a horny agricultural hand.

'Yes? . . . Prudence! What the hell are you doing telephoning me here. You're supposed to be spreading muck this afternoon. . . . What? . . . A fire? Jesus! A fire! Where? . . . Oh, that's not so bad. Have you telephoned the fire brigade? . . . Don't be so damn silly. Of course it's an emergency. Get on with it. I'll be home in a minute myself.' He slammed down the receiver. 'Stupid woman!' he muttered.

'What was that about, Kelvin?' asked the commander.

'Prudence,' he reported. 'She says the hay in the Dutch barn is on fire and she doesn't want to dial 999 in case it makes trouble. Women!' He returned to his drink.

The commander looked at him curiously. 'Aren't you concerned? If my property was on fire, I think I'd want to do a bit more than sit at a bar drinking beer.'

'There's bugger all I can do about it, Commander. If the

112

barn is burning, all I can do is piss on it. The fire brigade are the right people to deal with it. That's what they're there for and that's what we pay them for.'

'But it might spread. Prudence might do something silly and get hurt. Anything could happen.'

'No. The barn is well away from any other building.'

The only other proper agriculturalist present was Bill and he had known the ways of Kelvin for decades. 'What was your hay like this year, Kelvin?' he asked innocently.

Kelvin had his glass halfway up to his mouth but he paused to look suspiciously across at Bill. 'What's it to you?' he said.

'Nothing at all. Weren't you making hay that week in June when those two cows of Frank Mattock's were killed by lightning?'

'I might have been,' replied Kelvin cautiously.

'And you took weeks to repair the roof of your barn. It must have got very wet, your hay. Can't be much good.'

'Well, that's where you're wrong,' answered Kelvin. 'Best hay I've made for years. And the biggest crop.'

'It would be, wouldn't it?' said Bill. The civilians in the pub were not quite clear as to the purpose of this exchange, but Bill's next question threw a bit of light on the matter. 'You're well insured against fire, of course?' It was not so much the question, but the cynical chuckle that accompanied it. That, together with Kelvin's reaction.

He turned red. 'None of your bloody business!' he blared.

Bill was not fazed. 'If you want a bit of advice, Kelvin, you'd better be careful. We all know what you told Frank to do with his barn next to the new cottage.'

Kelvin looked briefly and contemptuously at Bill, but his reply was silenced by another volley of chirrups from the telephone. Helga picked it up, listened for a second and mutely stretched it out towards Kelvin a second time. Muttering under his breath in protest, he slid off his stool and came over to take it from her. 'What is it now?' he demanded. He listened for a few seconds. 'Yes, I know the barn is on fire,

113

you've already told me that. Has Mick arrived yet? . . . . He hasn't? Good!'

'What's good about that?' whispered the commander in some surprise.

'It's hay that's on fire,' replied Bill. 'When Mick shows up he's going to douse the lot in water which'll make it useless and leave Prudence to clear it all up. The more that's burned to ashes, the less there'll be to clear up.'

'I'm surprised Kelvin minds about giving Prudence extra work,' murmured the commander.

'He wants her to fell that wood on his southern boundary before it gets too wet to get a tractor down there, and it could take a week to clear up the hay if the fire brigade gets there too soon.'

'I see.'

'No!' shouted Kelvin suddenly. Conversation stopped as everyone turned to look at him. 'You'll do no such thing. It . . . er . . . would be too dangerous. Look, I'm coming straight home. Don't do anything until I get there.' He put down the telephone and hurried over to his pint and drained it with one draught. He slammed his empty glass down on the bar, belched and wiped the sleeve of his jacket across his lips. 'I'm off then,' he announced. 'Prudence is beginning to panic.'

'You mean she wants to put the fire out,' suggested Bill, getting to his feet. 'I'm coming along too.'

As it happened, the entire pub had been itching to rush up the road to Kelvin's farm so that they could see the fire, but it had seemed a little impolite to do so while the victim of this dramatic catastrophe continued to sit imperturbably at the bar. There was a general dash for the door.

A fire is one of life's most exciting spectacles. Kelvin's barn was a good fire, almost a great fire. There was a large pall of smoke towering up above the trees while the lane down to his farm was choked with the cars and Land Rovers of his neighbours who had come along to enjoy the thrills and the entertainment. The vehicles which brought the customers from the pub had to pull on to the verge near the top of the lane –

114

all except that belonging to Dennis whose passenger was Kelvin. He pulled out into the centre of the lane and parked across it. The vehicles emptied.

Dennis was not happy. 'What did you want me to park there for?' he demanded. 'Nobody else is going to be able to get in or out.'

'There looks to be quite enough people getting ghoulish pleasure from my disaster,' replied Kelvin as the group set off down the lane towards the smoke.

'He's no fool, our Kelvin,' contributed Bill. 'With your vehicle there, how is the fire engine going to get down?' Kelvin chose to ignore the remark. 'Incidentally, Kelvin, if you're hoping to persuade your insurers that you made decent dry hay, it's a pity that the smoke is so black.'

'What do you mean?' asked Kelvin.

'That's a very good point,' agreed the commander, pausing to pick up a nail lying on the grass hump in the middle of the lane and chuck it into the hedge. 'It's a bit like when they elect a pope. They use dry straw which makes white smoke when they've agreed on one and wet straw to make black smoke when they haven't.'

Kelvin looked at the great bank of smoke that was rolling down the narrow valley cutting through the farm. 'It's not all that black.'

'Any engineer officer would be proud if he could create a smoke screen of that density and that darkness,' scoffed the commander. 'You could hide the Grand Fleet behind it.'

The barn, with its open sides and rounded, corrugated-iron roof, stood about forty yards away from the house and the rest of the farm buildings. Watching it burn were about twenty human spectators, being fussed over by Percy, and about the same number of cattle. The latter were lining a field downwind of the crackling conflagration and their enthusiastic coughing when the smoke billowed over them would have been the envy of any concert audience.

Some of the barn's spectators had seen their fill of smoke and crackle and turned their backs on the fire to watch Prudence who had hitched a tractor to a venerable cast-iron

115

wagon, used to carry water into the fields in the days before water was piped to troughs. She had filled the wagon and was now snailing her way towards the barn. The interest lay in estimating the quantity of water that would be left by the time she reached her destination. At every bump and rut – and there were plenty of those about – the wagon lurched, sending a bucketful or a full-blown tsunami over the edge. There was also some discussion about her intentions, once she had reached her destination, between Frank Mattock and Gerald Mowbray, both farmers whose land ran with that of Kelvin.

'I reckon she's going to get the water out with a bucket,' said Gerald.

'Don't be daft. There's got to be 100 tons of hay there. Using a bucket would be like trying to shovel shit out of a cubicle shed with a teaspoon. Anyway, she wouldn't be able to get close enough. She'd fry in the heat.'

Gerald shook his head. 'She wouldn't fry, she'd more likely roast.' The wagon casually despatched a cubic foot of water at the back of Prudence's neck. 'Or boil. Perhaps she reckons she'll be protected from the heat by the amount of water on her.'

'No, she won't use a bucket. She must be going to tip it as close to the fire as she can get and try to swamp the flames.'

'That'd do no damn good, it'd just damp the outside of the bottom bales and, anyway, look at the state of the wagon,' argued Gerald. 'It won't have been tipped for nigh on fifty years. That tipping mechanism will have rusted solid. No woman is ever going to have the strength to shift it. Not even a woman like Prudence.' There was not a lot of Prudence, but what there was had earned the respect of the local agricultural community. 'Wiry' was a word that was often used to describe her, 'barbed wiry' by those who had come up against her in a deal for she had inherited her father's devotion to the cause of squeezing every penny out of every opportunity.

'You could shift it, Gerald,' said Frank. Gerald was a man of mighty thews. His speciality was flooring recalcitrant bullocks with a blow of his fist to the centre of the forehead.

'Shift what?' interrupted Kelvin. He had briefly inspected

116

the blazing barn and then surveyed the surrounding scene before coming to join his two fellow farmers.

'Oh, hullo, Kelvin, shame about your barn, but it was obviously a pretty awful bit of hay,' greeted Frank.

'Nice fire, though,' acknowledged Gerald.

'It was the best hay I've ever made,' said Kelvin indignantly.

'Best hay you've ever made!' jeered Frank. 'What the hell made it burst into flames if it was so damn good?'

'It was good,' insisted Kelvin.

'You're on a difficult one there, Kelvin,' said Gerald. 'Hay burns either because it's too wet when it's made or else because someone put a match to it. It's your choice, I suppose.'

'That's right. It's my choice. Hullo, Percy.'

Percy had seen Kelvin approach and had come hurrying over, looking important. Apart from Prudence, he was the only person present who seemed to think there was some kind of crisis going on. He shook his head worriedly. 'It's a bad business, this. It'll be another ten or fifteen minutes before the fire brigade gets here, I'm afraid.'

'Ten minutes!' said Kelvin with satisfaction. 'It'll be really blazing away by then.'

'That's right. They were called away to another fire, you see. It's just one of those things. Hay a bit damp, was it, Kelvin?'

'It damn soon will be unless I do something about Prudence. Excuse me a minute.' Prudence was creating something of a stir amongst the audience. She was in the process of negotiating a way through their ranks and the profligate behaviour of her water bowser was more than they had bargained for. Kelvin squelched through the mud towards her and tried to communicate over the crackle of the flames and the clatter of the tractor engine. She shook her head, leaned and cupped her ear. Kelvin raised his voice, looking irritated. She shook her head again. Kelvin took a deep breath and began to bellow.

Several small things happened simultaneously. Prudence decided to stop the tractor engine so that she could hear her

father. She did this economically, if in an unorthodox manner, by suddenly letting her foot off the clutch, thus inducing a stall. For a brief moment Kelvin was thoroughly audible. '— The insurance money, you stupid cow!' could be clearly heard for a fifty-yard radius. Percy pricked up his ears and sharply drew in his breath. Then the laws of physics relevant to the tractor's sudden halt came into inexorable effect. Kelvin watched helplessly as most of the remaining contents of the trailer rose four or five feet into the air and glittered in a brief moment of glorious existence against the low afternoon sun that managed to pierce the bank of black smoke before hurling itself accurately upon him.

The fire introduced a selection of alarming creaks to its repertoire of sounds as the heat began to take effect on the corrugated iron on the roof of the barn, but it had temporarily lost its position at the centre of the stage as its audience wiped tears of joy from their eyes at the sight of the spluttering Kelvin standing with the cargo of the cart cascading off him like meltwater from an iceberg. Even Prudence was moved to crack a rare smile as her father snorted water from his nostrils like a spouting dolphin, too surprised to show his customary fury. The only dissenter from the general delight was Percy. He had a gleam in his eye as he pushed through the revellers towards Kelvin, the words 'insurance money' still echoing in his ears. He pulled out a clean white handkerchief, neatly folded eight times as may well have been laid down in Police Regulations, and handed it to Kelvin. The latter, beginning to regain his composure, took it and dabbed his face briefly before dashing it to the ground and stamping it into the mud. Rage was clearly beginning to build.

Percy looked down at his handkerchief. 'You shouldn't have done that,' he said reproachfully. 'That handkerchief was police property.'

'What? A bloody police hankie? I'm sodden and you give me a hankie? What the hell's the good of that? If you're a bloody policeman, why don't you do your job? This lot here,' Kelvin spread his arms round at the crowd, 'they're all trespassers. Get rid of them. Everyone's laughing at me.'

'Trespass is a civil offence. You'd need a court order before I could do anything about it. Anyway, not everyone is laughing at you.'

'Yes, they are.'

'I'm not. I don't laugh at people when I'm on duty, especially when I'm investigating a possible offence.'

'Well, get on with it, then. I'm going to the house to get changed.' He turned to Prudence and shook his finger at her. 'And you let that fire well alone. It's not doing you any harm. So leave all the hero stuff to Mick and his lot, if they ever get here.'

'What were you saying to Prudence about insurance money just now?' asked Percy.

Kelvin turned from Prudence to Percy. 'What the hell is that to do with you?' he demanded. Kelvin never defended when he could attack.

The spectators had not only turned away from the fire but had also moved towards Kelvin and Percy and now surrounded them in a loose arc with the fire controlling the open side. 'He thinks that you started the fire for the insurance money, Kelvin,' Jimmy piped up. Jimmy was extremely old and it was quite understandable that he may have begun to lose his marbles. Even so, he had made a remarkably crass remark. The spectators wanted to hear if Percy would have the bottle to come out with the question himself and nobody wanted Jimmy to feed him his lines. There was some scornful tut-tutting and a bit of muttering and Jimmy looked a little abashed.

Percy turned to frown at him. 'I'd be grateful if you'd keep your mouth shut, Sir.'

The commander whispered in Gerald's ear, 'Sir? I've never heard him call Jimmy "Sir" before. He's being extremely official.'

Percy used his 'Sirs' in the old-fashioned country way. Those whom he considered gentry received them automatically and all other locals were known by their christian names. There was a speculative, almost wolfish gleam in most of the spectators' eyes, like the look in the eyes of a cat when it hears the first rustle in the wainscot and senses that the game's afoot. Kelvin picked up on it too. 'If you want to talk to me, Percy, you can come into the house because I'm not going to stand here and catch my death.' He stumped off in the direction of a set of dry clothes and, after a brief dither while he thought about his duty to protect the public from the dangers of immolation, Percy hurried off in pursuit of his first possible arsonist for at least a decade.

A fire, *per se*, is not enough. There needs to be human interest to add spice and hold the spectators' attention. If there is not the ultimate thrill of danger to person or persons, then it needs a distraught owner to stand around wringing his hands and being plangent or, at the very least, the possibility that it might spread. Kelvin had gone indoors; Prudence was trailing disconsolately back towards the tractor shed with her empty water cart; while the fire itself was settling down to chew its way steadily through the contents of the barn. Apart from a few rats which were scuttling out of the blaze as the heat reached more intimate areas of the pile of bales, there was precious little to get excited about. It was also after 3pm and there were chores to be done and no sign of anyone to bring out cups of tea.

Just as the audience was becoming restive with one or two of its members peeling away to trudge reluctantly back up the lane towards the road, the sound of a siren became intermittently audible above the fire. It brought Kelvin bounding back out of the house, hastily tying a piece of baler twine round his middle to keep his jacket closed. The fact that the jacket still had a full set of buttons on it was irrelevant as Kelvin was a traditionalist. Percy was in hot pursuit and neither of them seemed particularly happy.

'Get away from me!' snarled Kelvin over his shoulder. 'I'm buggered if I'm going to let someone else into my bedroom when I'm changing my trousers.'

'If you don't talk to me now, you'll have to talk to me down at the station,' replied Percy, puffing after him. 'Where do you think you're going?'

'Mind your own blasted business. Anyway you had no right to come into the house without a warrant.'

'Slow down,' commanded Percy. 'Where do you think you're off to?'

They made an odd couple. Kelvin was scuttling away from the fire across the yard, still trying to do up the buttons on his trousers. It looked as if he were heading for a small track that led towards Gerald Mowbray's farm.

'Gerald!' called Dennis from his shooting stick, on which he had parked himself. 'Have you any idea where Kelvin thinks he's going?'

'No idea,' replied Gerald, mystified. 'He may've gone round the twist.'

'How will we be able to tell the difference if he has?' asked Frank rather gloomily.

'Come on,' said Bill scornfully. 'You lot know Kelvin better than that. It's obvious, isn't it? He's making sure that Percy isn't around to clear the cars out of the lane so that the fire engine can get down.'

The stratagem was unsuccessful as Prudence was coming the other way, having put away the tractor. 'The fire engine's here, Father!' she yelled. Even Kelvin realized that it would look suspicious if he continued to run. He stopped and Percy stopped behind him, breathing rather heavily.

'What was that she said?' demanded Percy. Kelvin had no need to answer. The siren had stopped at the top of the lane but Mick must have switched it on again as he saw the obstructions. It blared out, its orchestrated cadences cutting through the disorganized crackle of the flames. Percy dithered again. He had Kelvin within his grasp and yet he was being summoned by the urgent demands of the siren.

'What was it that you wanted to ask me, Percy?'

'Sorry?' said Percy distractedly, his eye looking up the lane from where he was expecting the fire brigade to appear.

'I asked you what it was that you wanted to talk to me about. You've been chasing me for the last ten minutes.'

Percy turned back to him. 'Oh yes. I wanted to ask you about the insurance on the barn.' The siren sounded again. 'What's Mick up to?' asked Percy. 'Why doesn't he come down?'

'I don't know,' replied Kelvin. 'What about the insurance?'

Percy made his decision. 'It'll have to wait. I'd better go and see what's going on up the lane.'

'I may not want to talk to you later on,' said Kelvin sniffily.

Percy turned on the majesty of the Law. 'If I want to interview you later, I'll most certainly interview you later. And I'd be grateful if you did not leave the district until I've talked to you.' Kelvin gaped at him as he moved away. Percy paused and turned. 'Have you got a passport?'

'What the hell are you talking about, you silly bugger?' said Kelvin.

'Don't you call me a silly bugger, Kelvin Morchard. I just want to make sure you don't try to escape justice. We can't have you skipping off to South America or somewhere.'

'Well, you are a silly bugger. A piddling little fire in a hay barn and you're treating me as if I was a Great Train Robber. No wonder you failed your sergeant's exam so many times

122

that they wouldn't let you take it again! You haven't got enough brains in your head to police a church social!'

'Don't you dare talk to me like that!' cried Percy, raising his voice. 'You're not talking to *me*, you know. I'm on duty and you're talking to a policeman.'

'The policeman is talking like a bloody fool and he's on my property without my invitation or permission. I'm quite willing to talk to my friend Percy, but I'm damned if I'll give the time of day to an idiot like you.'

'You damn well watch yourself, Kelvin!' warned Percy through clenched teeth. 'You're playing with fire!'

Not surprisingly under the circumstances, this remark elicited a roar of laughter which did nothing to improve Percy's temper.

'I could have you here and now for insulting behaviour or . . . or conduct likely to cause a breach of the peace.'

The siren had been switched off but, above the noise of the fire, there was clearly heard a grinding sound which could only have been caused by the fire engine taking drastic steps to clear a path for itself.

'Bloody hell!' Dennis had risen from his shooting stick and stared up the lane before turning to Percy. 'For heaven's sake, stop messing around and go and do your job. That fire engine has just smashed up my Land Rover!'

Percy aimed one last shaft at Kelvin before returning to his duty. 'If you think you're going to get back in the skittle team, Kelvin, you've got another think coming!'

Kelvin jeered. 'If you think you're going to remain captain of the team, it's you who's going to get a surprise!'

'We'll finish this later,' stated Percy. He raised his voice to the assembled multitude. 'If anyone has a vehicle that is blocking the lane, now is the time to move it before it's moved for them.' Half a dozen spectators hurried across the yard, past the burning barn, with Percy following after them at a heavy trot. He was taking more exercise this afternoon than he was used to.

Kelvin turned back to look critically at the conflagration. 'What do you think, Frank?'

123

Frank looked as well. The fire was still doggedly going about its pre-ordained business, eating up the bales and smoking furiously. Within the last few minutes the flames had spread all over the surface of the hay, although much of it was obscured by smoke. Frank inspected it with an experienced eye. 'I should think you'll be OK. There doesn't seem much point in trying to put it out.'

'I hope you're right. But you know what Mick's like. Shall I get Prudence to make us a cup of tea?'

'You'd better have a word with Mick first. He'll be here in a minute.'

'Aye, I suppose I'd better.' They waited in companionable silence, watching the fire. Its quality of devotion to the task of ensuring its own death as quickly as possible by destroying its own means of existence excited some pity in Kelvin's stony heart. 'It would be a right shame if Mick spoilt it by pouring water all over it.'

'It makes such a filthy mess,' agreed Frank. 'And what's the use of a barn full of wet and smoky hay? Although I suppose it was already pretty damp before the fire started.' Kelvin failed to demur, so Frank continued, 'I must say, I don't quite know what Percy's going on about. It's obvious that the fire started because the hay was damp.' There was a speculative look in his eye as he stared at the flames. 'What's more to the point would be if you knew the hay was heating up and, if you did, whether the law says you should have done something about it.'

'Difficult one to prove, even if it was illegal. Percy's got no chance,' replied Kelvin.

At last the fire engine came roaring into the yard and its crew jumped off. Mick had a white helmet and those of his underlings were yellow, although the black tunic and yellow trousers he wore were similar to the others'. He stood with his hands on his hips and surveyed the scene. Kelvin and Frank came over.

Mick greeted them laconically. 'That piss-head Dennis is threatening to sue us for bashing up his Land Rover.'

'Us?' said Kelvin.

'Yes. You for telling him to park it in the middle of the lane and me for pushing it out of the way.'

'I see. And what has Percy got to say on the matter?'

'Not to worry. He wasn't there and my lads will say that the handbrake on the Land Rover was bust and it slid into the fire engine.' Mick would have made an excellent administrator for Big Brother. He believed that truth was entirely subjective and was what you wished to believe it to be. 'What do we do about this fire of yours, then? Have you got any chemicals or fertilizer in there?'

'Just hay. I think the best thing would be to let it burn out,' said Kelvin hurriedly.

'Insurance job?' queried Mick. 'Trying to get some decent hay in with the money?' He watched his minions unreeling their hoses, to Kelvin's increasing agitation. The stream that ran through the centre of his farm was about 100 yards from the burning barn and, with some degree of difficulty due to having been winkled out of a pub towards the end of their gorse fire, the firemen were linking hoses to reach over the fields towards it. 'Tricky one, that. Our job is to put out fires. Unless it's not worth it because of the risk to my lads. Very hot, hay fires. That roof'll be buckling soon. Could even begin to melt.'

'It looks very risky to me,' agreed Kelvin. 'Anyway, the fire's not doing anyone any harm and it would make a filthy mess if you tried to put it out. I'd be very grateful if you let it alone.'

Mick turned away from the fire towards Kelvin. 'Would you, now? Grateful. How grateful?'

Kelvin began to prevaricate. 'Well, you know, I'm not a rich man and with a disaster like this and—'

'—me listening in as well,' added Percy, who had joined them.

'This is nothing to do with you, Percy,' said Mick. 'Why don't you sod off and let the fire brigade deal with its own affairs?'

'I think that everything Kelvin's up to today is probably my affair. There's something very suspicious about the origins of this fire.'

'Suspicious?' mused Mick, turning back to the barn. 'Now there's a thing. Both you and Kelvin realize, of course, that it's my job to discover whether there is anything suspicious about it or not. It's a pity you're not rich, Kelvin.'

'It would be wrong to say I was poor, of course,' said Kelvin hurriedly. 'It all depends how you define rich.'

'That's easy,' replied Mick. 'Rich is the fellow who's got a bit more money than yourself. You, for instance, have a couple of hundred acres and a potential insurance settlement of several thousand pounds. I have only a cafe and a rather fierce wife.'

'She is pretty fierce,' agreed Kelvin. More and more local women were becoming tired of their roles as hewers of wood and drawers of water, which had been their lot since the Norman Conquest, to the baffled alarm of their menfolk whose culture and evolution had not equipped them to deal with a female sex that no longer recognized its secondary role. 'I miss the wife, God rest her soul, but I'm quite glad that I'm a widower. Prudence does for me fine.'

'You wouldn't catch me with a wife,' agreed Percy. 'My mother does for me.'

'—And her scones are quite something. You don't need a wife if you've got a mother who can make scones as good as hers. My Prudence makes a very nice fruit cake, but she's no good at scones.'

Percy had an idea. 'If I got my mother to make scones for you, would you exchange them for clotted cream?' Kelvin looked dubious. 'Go on,' continued Percy coaxingly. 'It would be fair exchange. You've got cows and lots of cream and I've got the scones.'

'We sell scones and clotted cream in the cafe,' contributed Mick hopefully. 'You could always come round to us. They're only 95p for two.'

'People?' asked Percy.

'No, scones.'

Percy weighed up the possibilities. He sighed. 'It's not the same, though, is it? The whole point of scones and clotted cream is that you have lots of cream left over and can dip your

126

finger into the bowl and lick it. Your Beryl does individual portions of jam and cream and the tourists don't know any better. I'd rather do a trade with Kelvin.'

'You sound as though you're talking about a lot of cream,' said Kelvin dubiously, conscious of time passing and flames flaming. 'How do you reckon we might work it? How many scones to how much cream? After all, although your mother's scones are better than most, they don't cost very much. It's the cream that pushes up the price. Isn't that right, Mick?'

'That's right,' confirmed Mick. 'I buy my cream from Ivor and he charges a shocking price.'

'That's one of the reasons I don't come to the cafe,' explained Percy. 'He's got Friesian cows and you really want good thick Jersey cream. Nice and yellow with the consistency of cold treacle.'

'My cows aren't Jerseys,' said Kelvin.

'Your cows aren't anything in particular, but I had a look in the tank at the top of your lane and the milk looked nice and yellow.'

'What the hell were you doing poking your nose into my milk tank?' demanded Kelvin. 'And when was it?'

'Last week some time. It's my job to know what goes on in the parish. It could have been anything in your tank.'

'Anything? What the hell do you expect to find in a milk tank except milk?'

'I heard of one farmer who stuffed the body of his dead wife into his milk tank,' said Percy darkly.

Kelvin and Mick looked at him incredulously. 'That's as bloody silly a story as I've ever heard!' snorted Kelvin. 'Nobody would do a thing like that. If you stuck a body in a tank, you'd have all your milk rejected by the dairy as sure as fate. And another thing, if I have any trouble with the dairy in the next day or two about my milk, I'll tell them it was you opening up the lid and dropping your bogeys into it. If they complain about poor hygiene, I'll tell them to take it up with you.'

During this dissertation on the art of scones and clotted cream, the fire crew had succeeded in linking their hoses to the stream and were waiting for Mick to give them the word. He recalled his duty. 'Well, I suppose we might as well get on with putting out this fire of yours, Kelvin.'

'I'd much rather you didn't,' implored the latter. 'It's doing nobody any harm and it'll burn itself out in a couple of hours.'

'You get on and do your duty, Mick,' contributed Percy pompously. 'You've got my backing if there is any come-back.'

Mick sighed, looking apologetically at Kelvin. 'I'm sorry, Kelvin. Look at it from my point of view.' He gestured towards the firemen and the rest of the spectators. 'This lot all want me to put it out. My lads like nothing better than a nice, straightforward barn fire. All those people watching are expecting it of me and that great nit' – he indicated Percy – 'has every intention of being awkward if we do nothing.'

'Bloody right I do!' said Percy with relish. 'There's something definitely suspicious about this here fire and Kelvin's attitude.'

'How about if I got on the phone to the insurance company and they said it was all right to let it burn out?' asked Kelvin desperately.

'Don't be daft,' replied Mick. 'No insurance company's going to say that.'

'At least let me try,' responded Kelvin. 'Look, just give me a couple of minutes on the phone and then you can spray water as much as you like.'

Mick thought for a few seconds. 'OK, Kelvin, you've got two minutes and then my lads'll get on with it.'

'Here!' cried Percy. 'You can't do that. You start squirting your bloody hoses right now.'

'Look, Percy, I've told you already: I don't tell you how to do your job and you don't tell me how to do mine,' said Mick patiently. 'Two minutes is neither here nor there.'

Percy knew he could not shift Mick so he turned to Kelvin. 'No nonsense, mind. If your insurance man says yes, I'll want to talk to him.' Percy had had to raise his voice as Kelvin had already dived into the house. 'Silly old bugger,' muttered Percy after his retreating back. Mick went over to the lads to explain the situation to them and to discuss their tactics once they went ahead with their extinguishing. A stir of expectation ran through the crowd, which had begun to become slightly restive due to the inaction of the fire brigade. Even the spectating cattle kicked up their heels in excitement and careered briefly round their field before coming back to a snorting halt along the fence.

Percy placed himself in the porch of the farmhouse studying his watch, ready to burst through the door as soon as the time was up, but Kelvin appeared in the doorway with fifteen seconds still to go, brushed his way past without giving him a glance and walked slowly out into the yard towards the fire engine. Every eye was on him.

Percy came pattering after him. 'Well?' he demanded. 'What did he say?'

Kelvin stopped. 'I am not telling you anything. I'm going to tell Mick. It's nothing to do with you.'

'He said no, didn't he?' jeered Percy.

'It's none of your business,' replied Kelvin firmly.

'He said no. Don't deny it. That'll teach you!' It was not often that one could see a policeman in uniform actually dancing with glee, but Percy was capering in front of Kelvin rather like a large puppy. Kelvin looked at this exhibition with phlegmatic distaste, showing no inclination to go over to let Mick into the insurance company's decision. So Mick came across to find out the news for himself.

'Well?' he demanded.

'Well what?' asked Kelvin innocently.

'He said no. Go on, admit it. He said no,' crowed Percy.

'He said nothing of the sort,' replied Kelvin.

Percy paused in mid-caper, one leg poised rather ludicrously. His face showed first dismay, then incredulity, then anger. 'Balls! I don't bloody believe you. He said yes?' Kelvin opened his mouth to reply, but Percy did not give him a chance to speak. 'Anyway, you can go and phone him right back. If you remember, I said I would want to hear for myself, and by the time I've had my say he'll be saying no or I'll resign from the bloody force.' Kelvin made to say something again. 'Go on.

129

Admit it. You're lying. I don't believe he said any such thing.'

'Percy, why the hell don't you shut up and let Kelvin speak?' said Mick mildly. Percy shut up and the two of them looked expectantly at Kelvin. The latter glanced from one to the other.

'Well?' demanded Percy.

If Kelvin was about to say anything, which looked fairly unlikely, it would have been drowned by a double blast from the siren on the fire engine. It made everyone from Percy to the smallest of the watching cattle jump. 'Jesus!' exclaimed Mick, turning on his heel to glare at the fireman in the cab. 'What the hell does he think he's up to?' The figure in the cab was gesticulating wildly. Mick trotted the few yards across to the fire engine.

Percy, breathing heavily, glared from Kelvin to Mick to Kelvin again. Everyone else was now looking at Mick who listened briefly to his man in the cab and then signalled to the rest of the crew who hurriedly began to reel in their hoses. He strode back to Percy and Kelvin. 'It looks as though you're off the hook, Kelvin. There's been a 999 call about a grass fire up on the moor.'

Percy was aghast. 'You can't go away and leave this because of some bloody grass fire. It's been pouring with rain the last day or two anyway.'

'The bloke who phoned up said that he and his family were on a picnic and the fire had them surrounded.'

'Nobody has a picnic at this time of year and, anyway, if the fire had them surrounded, how did he get to a telephone?'

'He said he just happened to have one of those new-fangled radio telephones in his car.'

'What a load of nonsense!' said Percy angrily.

'I know,' agreed Mick. 'The chances are it is a hoax call, but we can't afford to risk it. We never can. Think what would happen if we left a family of tourists to burn! It would be lousy for business. If you'll excuse me.' Mick was off. The hoses were reeled in; the lads stood on the running board like Keystone cops, steeled their jaws, and looked into the middle distance as the fire engine engaged gear. Blue light flashing and siren blaring, it roared off up the lane, spraying a plume of mud and cowdung from under its wheels.

Percy turned, slitty-eyed with frustration, to Kelvin. 'You jammy bastard! That insurance man told you to put the fire out didn't he?'

'I couldn't find his number, so I didn't get through to him.'

'Who did you phone then?'

'I didn't phone anyone.'

Jimmy still had not learned to keep his mouth shut. 'Yes you did, Kelvin. I heard the bell out in the yard tinkle. You must have used the phone.' Most of the farms had outside bells so that the farmer could hear the telephone ring when he was out ministering to his beasts. Percy looked puzzled; the rest of the spectators merely frowned at Jimmy.

'Who were you on the phone to, Kelvin? Percy asked.

'I must have jogged the receiver with my sleeve when I was trying to find the insurance man's number,' replied Kelvin innocently.

Percy knew Kelvin well enough to realize that the given explanation was almost certainly not the correct one, but he was not a lateral thinker. Everyone, including Kelvin, looked curiously at him, wondering when he might manage to add two and two together. Percy darted glances at his onlookers, trying to work out why he was the object of so many pairs of eyes. He rubbed his chin thoughtfully, his mind ruminating gently over all the inputs that had recently come its way. The fire might as well have given up and gone out for all the attention that it was getting.

'Very nice for you, Kelvin, that Mick was called away,' said Percy. The audience held its breath. 'I bet it was a hoax call. These bloody kids are a real pain.' Jimmy began to moan softly. He had understood at last and the tension created by the ponderous workings of Percy's brain cells was getting to him. He shut up when Gerald Mowbray kicked him on the ankle. Suddenly it happened. All the cogs fell into place with such force that Percy's head jerked to one side under their impact. 'Christ Almighty! That telephone call to the fire brigade. It was you who made it, wasn't it, Kelvin?' His denial was inaudible beneath the muted cheer from the gallery. 'What?' demanded Percy.

'I said no. I didn't telephone anybody.'

'You're a lying bastard! Of course it must have been you. It's just too convenient. What kind of an idiot do you take me for?'

Rhetorical questions of that nature are most unwise. Kelvin looked slowly round at the audience who were daring him to come out with the truth. When it suited his own interests, however, Kelvin knew exactly how to play things. 'I made no telephone call, Percy. Even if I had done, which I did not, there is absolutely no way that you could prove it was me. I bet it isn't a false alarm, anyway. There probably is a fire up at Higher Down.'

Gerald Mowbray opened his mouth. 'Higher Down? Who said anything about Higher Down?' Kelvin heard Gerald Mowbray and turned a delicate shade of grey. Everyone else heard Gerald Mowbray and held their breath – everyone, that is, save Percy. He was busy on another track.

'I'll prove it if it's the last thing I ever do!' he roared. 'I'll trace the telephone call. I'll make voice prints. Nobody can make a fool of me like that. Just you wait, Kelvin Morchard. I'll get you.'

'Oh, go to hell, Percy. If you can catch me, then do what the hell you like, but until then go away and stop wasting my time.'

'Right!' said Percy, breathing heavily. 'Right! I'll be off now. But I'll be back. Mark my words, I will return.'

'You and Fu Manchu,' replied Kelvin, ensuring that he had the last word. Percy, his lips tight with frustration, turned on his heel and stalked off up the lane towards his bicycle and his mother's scones.

The fire was left to its own devices for the rest of the afternoon and early evening while people went home to catch up on their chores. They reassembled after dark when Kelvin broke out several bottles of his home-made wine for a fire party and the spectators, who included half of the crew of the fire tender, caroused on into the evening, seated on barrels,

warming their toes on the gently decaying barn. They watched the sparks floating into the air while the bats flitted in and out of the firelight, harvesting moths and other insects attracted by the abnormal brightness and warmth in the autumnal evening. The cattle lay down along the fence to cud, their eyes reflecting the glow of the embers.

'It was a damn good fire even if Mick didn't put it out,' said Dennis, belching contentedly.

'Bit of luck about that hoax call,' added the commander.

'That reminds me!' exclaimed Mick. 'The emergency operator asked the caller for his number.'

'They always do,' agreed the commander.

'That's right, they always do. Anyway, the number the caller gave was yours, Kelvin.'

There was silence, broken only by a soft thump as the ghost of a hay bale rolled over, jetting sparks into the sky.

The commander sighed. 'Ah well, nobody can remember everything.'

'I put Percy off when he asked about it,' said Mick.

'Some say otherwise, Mick, but I've always maintained

you're a decent sort of a bloke,' said Kelvin, looking deep into the fire.

'That's nice of you to say so, Kelvin.'

'And I'm sure I can find a bit of cream for you now and again. Really cheap.'

'That'd be right neighbourly of you,' replied Mick.

Chapter Nine

'IS IT HARDY, dear?' asked Elfrieda eagerly as her husband
fine-sprayed coffee across the inside back page of *The Times*.
The commander was wont to chortle or sigh occasionally over
breakfast as he perused the deaths column, but a snort of such
proportions could only mean a demise of outstanding quality,
possibly even that of the retired admiral whose adverse report
had caused the untimely end of his career. The commander
had been racked by jealousy when he had discovered that
even the densest of his contemporaries now sported an MVO
for elbowing an impertinent *paparazzo* off a jetty during one of
the honeymoons spent on the royal yacht.

'No,' replied her husband. 'It's us!'

'What? Us in the obituaries! What are you talking
about?'

'No, we're not dead. It's this advertisement under "Holidays
and Villas". It mentions the village! It's got our phone
number. I mean, it's a local number.'

'Whose is it?'

'137.'

'137? That's Mrs Baggins!'

'No, she's 127. Who on earth could it be?'

'Well, read the blasted advert and find out, then!' Her
increasing shortness with him the commander put down to
feminism rather than to his own growing preference for nursing
beer in the pub over that for nursing his seedlings. He threw
her a dirty look above the top of the paper.

'I was just about to, dear.' He cleared his throat. ' "Find
yourself in beautiful surroundings." '

'Well? Don't stop.'

'That's all there is. That and the phone number. What do you think it could mean?'

'It's a mistake. They must have left out a line.'

'No, they can't have done. Surroundings is on two lines, although I suppose the word could be surrender. "Find yourself in beautiful surrender in our fascinating surroundings." Perhaps it's someone trying to advertise bed and breakfast. Imaginative use of our native tongue is not a notable local characteristic.' His face lit up. 'No! Of course! It must be the communards. Find yourself in the sense of finding your soul, like Kelvin said he did when he looked down the barrel of that poacher's gun when he was a special constable.'

'But the communards haven't got a phone.'

'Oh. Well, who on earth could it be?'

'Ring up and find out.'

The commander shook his newspaper nervously. 'I couldn't just ring up. It would be frightfully rude.'

'They wouldn't have published their phone number in the personal column if they didn't want to be phoned up,' responded Elfrieda reasonably.

'Yes, but not by neighbours. They could have stuck up a notice in the post office window if they wanted us to phone. I'll ask in the pub at lunchtime. Someone there is bound to have rung up to find out by then.'

'The only problem is that most of that lot have enough trouble when it comes to reading the *Sun*. They certainly won't have read *The Times*.'

'Don't worry. The advert could be etched on a microchip placed on the dark side of the moon and the village would know ten minutes after sunset.'

It was Saturday and so there was a good turnout of locals enjoying the sight of Helga trying to explain to a family of foreigners that their six-year-old could not be served with a drink, when the commander bustled importantly into the pub. He waited until the bewildered guttural noises that the visitors were making faded as Helga shut the door behind them before

136

he made his announcement. He thought he would start quietly.

'By the way, whose phone number is 137?'

'You been looking at that advert? It's bloody silly if you ask me,' replied Kelvin.

'Oh.' The commander felt decidedly deflated. 'Whose is it, then?'

'It's the Jarretts. Malcolm's organizing a weekend on the moor. He said they're camping out so that they can tune into their essence, but it's bound to rain. I told him that there was no point putting an advert up in the post office because nobody from round here is going to do anything like that. He's charging £12.50 too!'

'I actually saw it in *The Times* this morning.'

'I mean, who's going to pay £12.50 to walk on the moor when they can do it for nothing?'

'I can't imagine,' replied the commander gloomily.

'And who would want to go there even if they could do it for free? It's just steep ground, bogs and scrub. You'd have to drain and lime it before you could plough and it just wouldn't be worth the expense.'

' "Heather and a rolling landscape with wooded combes" is what they call it in the tourist brochures,' murmured the commander.

'You go looking for missing sheep up there and you'd soon find the place is one of God's mistakes. It's only good for breaking the necks of tourists.'

'It would do you good to take a weekend in the open air, Kelvin.'

'Couldn't do it, even if I wanted to. It's the beginning of Operation Bulldog that weekend.'

'Operation Bulldog?' inquired the commander.

'That's right,' replied Kelvin importantly. 'All the nation's defences are on full alert and we're practising for when the Russians invade. As head of the Emergency Volunteers, I'm commandeering Gerald Mowbray's bacon wireless.'

'Don't tell me. Let me guess,' said Lindy.

Kelvin looked mystified. 'What's with you?'

'I know, Commander!' exclaimed Lindy delightedly. 'Ham radio! Oh, that's a real goody, Kelvin.'

Kelvin shrugged. 'Yeah, that's it. His farm is going to be my command post.'

Malcolm marketed his weekend with subtlety. He knew that, faced with a phalanx of cynical faces in the pub, he would have no luck at all. On the telephone he could isolate prospects and flatter. 'Commander, I was hoping you might come along next weekend on this stroll I'm organizing.'

'Actually, I was hoping to watch *Dynasty* on Friday—'

'—We need a man of your skills and experience along with us. There'll be some young ladies who will be very grateful to you if you come.'

'Young ladies? Grateful to me?'

'For your money you get a free breakfast every morning and we've got a carefully planned itinerary.'

'Young ladies? Have you ... er ... met any of them? They're not like Mandy, are they?'

'Lord, no. They're really nice people. Lovely figures, too.'

'Well, in that case, I might be able to manage it. I can always get *Dynasty* videoed by Ivor.'

'He's coming too.'

'Is he, by God! It was just the young ladies, I bet. Ha ha. Do I have to bring a sleeping bag? I'm a bit past that sort of thing, you know.'

'Ho ho,' concurred Malcolm. 'Come along on Friday at about 10pm. Just bring yourself and some sensible clothes. Everything else has been taken care of.'

'Sounds quite fun. Bags I a bed in with the young ladies, eh?'

'It's a men-only weekend. But the wives will be very pleased that a man of your calibre will be going along. See you Friday. Bye.'

'Shit!' said the commander as he slammed down the telephone.

'What's wrong with you?' asked Elfrieda who was passing

138

through the hall bearing some tobacco leaves, part of their latest crop, towards the airing cupboard.

'I've been conned into going on this weekend that Malcolm's running.'

'That'll be nice. I'll be able to have a couple of days to myself. I might throw a party.'

'Well, don't count on many men being around. Half the male population of the village will be off on the moor before Malcolm is finished.'

In the event only the commander, Ivor and Keith turned up at the Jarretts' cottage on a wet Friday night. The commander and Ivor were dressed almost identically in Barbour jackets, corduroy trousers and green gumboots. The only variation was the commander's choice of a deerstalker as opposed to Ivor's flat cap. Keith wore a blue nylon padded anorak and black gumboots. Malcolm greeted them at the door. They noticed uneasily that he was sporting knee breeches and the heavy woollen socks that are worn by the active variety of tourist who is usually enveloped above his calves in an orange kagoule that rustles and crackles like the sails on a storm-driven windjammer as he tramps his way through the village, his eyes fixed on the cloud-covered moor a mile or two beyond.

'Come in, come in,' greeted Malcolm cordially, ushering them in. Both he and his wife went jogging and swallowed lots of authentically dull food purveyed in large brown paper bags by a shop that still called itself 'Health' rather than 'Whole'. This made them both look fit but Kelvin had observed that it seemed to cause them to belch and fart a good deal, although the former appeared to be a necessary part of their culture as the eructations were emitted with pride.

The visitors filed through into the sitting room which had been laid out with the sofa and chairs lined up facing one way and lines of cushions on the floor. 'Sit down, please.' Malcolm indicated the sofa and they sat themselves nervously down on the oatmeal hessian covers. Malcolm took the chair opposite, from where he could control the meeting, and stared pleasantly at them.

139

After half a minute's silence, the commander cleared his throat: 'Harrumph!' Malcolm continued to look benign while Ivor and Keith turned to the commander, expecting him to say something to break this rather odd quiet. The commander picked up their vibrations. 'Have you got anything to drink?'

'It wouldn't be wise.'

'Oh.' There was another hiatus. 'How many people are you expecting?'

'Twenty-three.'

'And what exactly are we going to do?'

'Let's wait until everyone's here and then I'll tell you – there again, perhaps I won't.' Malcolm smiled enigmatically. Ivor yawned theatrically, picked up a magazine from the top of a pile on the polished wooden floor, which was scattered tastefully with numdah rugs, and put it back down again when he saw that it was a copy of *Alliance News*.

'Are we allowed to talk?' asked Keith.

'Of course,' smiled Malcolm. 'You can do what you like until everyone else comes.'

'Good. What exactly is the point of this weekend? You were rather vague about it on the phone.'

'Yes,' agreed Ivor. 'I'm not sure—'

'I'd rather we waited until the others are here before we talk about what we're going to do,' interrupted Malcolm. 'It will save saying everything twice.'

There was another short silence. 'Where's Stephanie?' asked the commander.

'I sent her away for the night.'

'Gosh!' exclaimed the commander admiringly. He would no more dare send his wife out for the night than wear a tie with a Windsor knot.

Malcolm reddened. 'Actually, she wanted to go out. She's gone to the theatre with some friends from work.'

The silence stretched to twenty minutes before the doorbell rang. Ivor put away the hoof knife that he used in idle moments to scrape the accumulations of mud, dung and tractor oil from beneath his finger nails and looked up expectantly as Malcolm went off to answer its summons.

140

There was a tramping in the hall and a trio of bespectacled men of around thirty entered the room. They had the same woolly socks as Malcolm and all carried rucksacks which they placed on the floor. The bell rang again and the room gradually filled. The locals, recipients of curious looks from the others, huddled together on the sofa, as a murmur of conversation in half a dozen accents from Newcastle southwards discussed mountains they had conquered, mighty expeditions they had endured across barren plateaux and argued the merits of various types of dubbin for their supple boots.

Malcolm called the meeting to attention. 'Right!' he said briskly. 'I didn't get anyone from our advert, although there were a few phone calls, but this weekend we're going to tune into our emotional strengths. We're going to strip away all the dross of civilization and tap into the essence of our collective manhood.'

There were excited 'rhubarb' noises from the bulk of the congregation while the commander's murmur of 'Heavens!' earned him a few dirty looks from those close enough to hear.

'In a few minutes, we shall be splitting you up into groups of five and then you will be making a night march to a pre-arranged rendezvous point.'

'But it's pouring with rain!' exclaimed Ivor.

'It'll make it all the more interesting,' said Malcolm.

'Where will we sleep?' asked the commander.

'You won't tonight,' said Malcolm cheerfully, 'unless you get to the rendezvous point early, which is in a nice warm barn.'

'Good God!'

'There are also a couple of wobblies that we'll be throwing at you. You will not be told where you're being dropped and myself, Peter here' – a man with smoothly swept-back blond hair and an out-of-season tan smiled coldly – 'and Tom' – Tom had the sleek, doctored-cat look of someone who prospered undemandingly in the City – 'will be touring round the area all night and, if we catch you, you will be dumped five miles further away from the rendezvous point.'

141

Before the three locals had been able to do more than exchange looks, let alone confer in private when they would have been able to give each other the courage to walk out and return to their nice warm beds, Malcolm read out the names of the groups, bracketing Ivor with the commander but allowing Keith to fall among strangers. The party adjusted their kagoules and tightened the laces on their books. Leaving the cottage they obediently boarded vehicles and were driven away into the leaden, moonless night.

There is a unique desolation of the soul which comes in the depths of the English countryside when a motorist *perdu* reaches a crossroads and finds that he has has heard of none of the four villages to which the signpost points. Being ejected from a vehicle into stormswept darkness with one feeble torch for illumination conjured up much the same in sensation in Ivor's group, particularly when a ten-minute grope revealed that they were at a crossroads without any signpost at all.

Ivor and the commander made straight for shelter and stood disconsolately beneath the drips of a scrubby hedgerow while the experienced weekenders discussed the matter in whispers from the other, exposed, side of the lane.

'Turn on the torch so that I can read the map,' ordered one of their companions, Roy from Huddersfield in a yellow anorak.

'If we turn on the torch, the patrols might see us and we'll be caught,' replied another. Judging by the area of dark from which his voice emanated, the commander decided that it must have been Hugh who was about 5 feet high with a face like a piglet. Hugh came from London. 'And anyway, if we get the map out, it'll probably disintegrate in the rain and then we really will be in the shit.'

'We'll just have to risk it. We won't get very far if we have to stand here all night and we've been dumped with these two. Have you seen their feet? They've got gumboots on.' That was the third who was tall and thin with boots so supple with use that one could see his toes wriggle beneath the leather in a manner that seemed faintly obscene. The map was unfolded; the torch gave light and a conference ensued.

142

'Have you got any whisky on you?' muttered the commander to Ivor as the cough of a sheep in the field behind their hedge distracted the experts into twittering excitement.

'What was that?'

'It's Malcolm!'

'It's not fair! We can't be caught already. Quick! Put out the torch! Everyone into the ditch!' Three dark shapes rushed past the commander and Ivor. It had been heavy rain and it was a main ditch, so the water was a foot deep over a muddy bottom. They made quite a splash.

'I've only got one bottle. What are these people doing in the ditch? And why are you whispering?' asked Ivor.

'I've only got one as well. I'm whispering because I bet these people have got none at all and I don't want to dissipate it and I've no idea what they're up to in the ditch.'

'Sshh!' hissed the ditch.

The commander sneezed. The sheep coughed again. There was consternation. 'That's torn it!' said Hugh, the piggy one, savagely. 'I knew we'd drawn the short straw with these two in our group!'

'Excuse me!' said the commander to the ditch politely. 'What are you doing?'

'We're hiding.'

'Why? I thought we were supposed to be going to that barn.'

Another sheep bleated. Sheep do not all say 'meeah' – if they did, they would all sound the same, which would remove the only point of making the noise at all. Some sheep howl, some yelp, some squawk, some sound like the most derelict of winos trying to hawk phlegm from the wreckage of his lungs, and some sound like Mrs Thatcher. This particular animal had a mellow growl.

There was a muttered conversation from the ditch. Then the sound of them hauling themselves out. Eyes were becoming used to differentiating between sky-dark and the padded-cell blackness below the horizon and the three silhouettes were visible above the line of the hedge.

'All right, Malcolm! We give in!' shouted Hugh, as the sheep growled once more.

'Oh, I see!' exclaimed Ivor. 'There's no need to worry. That's just a sheep.'

'A sheep?'

'A sheep.'

'That's not a sheep, that's a human voice,' stated Hugh patronizingly.

'Meeah!' said another voice in the accents of an ovine Richard Burton.

'Oh. Well, all I can say is that you've got some bloody funny-sounding sheep down here.'

'We probably have,' responded Ivor equably. He would quite happily defend his purse, his daughter's innocence and possibly even his nation from verbal abuse, but sheep noises could look after themselves. 'How long do you want to stand around here, by the way?'

'Until we know where we are. We don't want to set off in the wrong direction, do we?'

'Why don't we find out where we are then?'

'We can't. We don't know where we are on the map.'

'Give me the torch,' ordered Ivor. It was passed over and he flashed his way a few yards down the lane to a gateway and shone it through. He gave a grunt of satisfaction. 'That's not too bad. It shouldn't take us more than a couple of hours to walk to the barn. The moor's a couple of hundred yards up this lane and we can pick up a footpath there. Shall we get going?' Ivor strode briskly off into the darkness.

The commander joined him, but the others showed reluctance. 'How do you know all that from looking through a gate?' shouted Hugh suspiciously.

Ivor turned and called back, 'I recognized the grass. If you live in the country, you grow to know different grass like you people in towns recognize buildings.'

'Oh.' There was a note of surprised respect in Hugh's voice and they followed in silence along the tarmac road surface.

The commander mulled things over for a few hundred dark yards. 'You didn't really recognize the grass, did you?' he whispered.

'It was the sheep,' replied Ivor.

'You asked the sheep?'

'In a manner of speaking. They're Dick Hunniford's which means that the field must be his fifteen-acre meadow.'

'You can tell who owns a sheep just by looking at it? That's just about as good as recognizing grass.'

'It's not difficult when there's a large 'DH' in blue dye on their backs,' replied Ivor mildly.

It was a gentle if soggy stroll across the edge of the moor to the rendezvous point which was reached by 3am. They enjoyed a peaceful few hours amid the hay bales.

Peter decided to make a move at 6.30. He walked over to the barn, his hair gleaming in the watery morning sunshine, to stand looking up into the dim heap of bales. 'Right, everyone out!'

'Is breakfast ready?' demanded the commander after Peter had shouted for some time. He peered down, showing little inclination to move.

'No.'

'I'm not getting up until it's breakfast time. Here!' he said accusingly, 'you've had a shave! If you were scouring the lanes for us all night, when did you have time to shave? I bet you've had a bath too.'

145

'I haven't.

'You twister! I can smell your Essence of Athlete aftershave from here.'

There were murmurings of support from the other three but it was *sotto voce* as they had no desire to face court martial for insubordination. Peter was not prepared to surrender authority to the contents of the barn.

'You have thirty seconds to come down or there will be no breakfast for you,' he ordered.

In spite of the threat, it was a good twenty-five seconds before the incipient mutiny crumbled and the three slid down the hay bales with the commander and Ivor following more circumspectly behind. Another of the groups, whose members had arrived later on, clambered down from the eaves at the other end of the barn. They drew up in a ragged line opposite Peter who regarded them coldly. He had his hands behind his back and bounced gently on his toes. 'I think you lot need a bit of exercise before breakfast.' There was a chorus of groans. 'Everyone into the orchard behind the barn. Hugh, come and help me carry stuff from the camper.'

Ten disconsolate people, most of them tired, gritty, wet and potentially foul-tempered, trailed through the nettles and long grass into the orchard to a roughly scythed circle where they stood to watch Hugh, playing teacher's pet, and Peter carry in a large rug-covered bundle which they dropped on the ground with a clatter.

Peter put an arm inside and drew out a long sword. Ivor and the commander exchanged a wary glance as Peter flexed his arm with the authority of the Black Prince before Crécy. 'Steve!' he called. 'Let's have a bit of a warm-up.'

Steve was tall, fair and bearded. He pushed his way through and selected a sword, waving it above his head. His resemblance to a Viking berserker was marred only by his pebble-lens spectacles. His sword, like the others, was a piece of roughly shaped wood about a yard long with a crosspiece at the hilt. Before the wondering gaze of the commander and Ivor they came on guard, saluted and circled each other before emitting screams of rage and falling on one another,

146

parrying and thrusting at each other's vitals.

'Jesus wept!' exclaimed the commander. 'What on earth do they think they're up to?'

'It's duelling with English broadswords,' explained Hugh. 'Peter thought it up on a weekend in the Yorkshire Dales. It's purpose is to put you in touch with your male aggression.'

'Is that so?' remarked the commander, wincing as Peter rattled Steve's ribs with a slashing swipe that the latter failed to avert. He continued to watch, open-mouthed, as the contestants, who were now breathing heavily, clattered their wooden blades while they slashed away with no apparent concern for each other's wellbeing.

The commander started violently when Ivor nudged him in the ribs just as Steve did the same to Peter. Ivor nodded towards the roadside where Father Loosemire, just beginning his letter round, was peering over the hedge from the roof of his van to discover the source of these hoarse cries and the peculiar clattering sound. 'Hell!' said the commander as he and Ivor moved smartly behind the trunk of a gnarled apple. 'We'll be a laughing stock in the village if he recognizes us.'

After a couple of minutes it became clear that Peter's sword-play would prove decisive. He had a determined grin on his face, baring his teeth like Errol Flynn, as he drove Steve back with successive blows until the latter slipped to fall flat on his back, the sword spinning from his hand. Peter prodded him in the belly, driving the breath from his vanquished opponent and held the tip of the sword against his heaving chest. For a dreadful moment, both the commander and Ivor thought that Peter had regressed to Hammer Horror and was about to skewer Steve as one would a vampire. They would have leaped forward to protect him had not a hee-hawing laugh from Father Loosemire over the hedge reminded them of the wisdom of preserving their anonymity. The laugh also broke into the battle haze clouding the brain beneath Peter's hair which was still sleek with an emulsion of sweat and brilliantine. He turned towards the hedge with a snarl, lifting the sword above his head. The commander feverishly wondered what was appropriate: not a Tarzan yell, not 'All for One and

147

One for All', nor even 'God for Harry! England and St George!' Peter must have been wondering as well since he opened and shut his mouth a few times before merely managing a hoarse roar. It was enough for Father Loosemire. Uttering a cry of alarm, he scurried into his van before this lunatic could attack and roared off down the lane, his mind busily honing and polishing the experience into an anecdote that would absorb the discerning audience of the pub.

'Right!' said Peter. 'That's how you do it.' His eyes swept the watchers. Ivor had stepped out from behind the tree with the disappearance of the post office van but the commander, an older campaigner, elected to stay where he was. This defence was sufficient to protect him from a casual inspection, but Peter's eye carefully winkled him out. 'You!' he barked, extending the point of his sword straight at the commander. 'Come out here and have a go!'

The commander needed no more than a split-second to consider his response. 'No.'

'Come on,' repeated Peter impatiently. 'I won't hurt you. You'll be all right, won't he, Steve?'

'He'll be fine,' groaned Steve, using a fallen branch to haul himself to his feet while one hand protectively hugged his battered ribcage.

The commander laughed incredulously. 'There is absolutely no chance of me hitting someone else with those ridiculous weapons. Or being hit myself.'

'They're not ridiculous!' said Malcolm who had come down to observe. 'We've been using them for years and they really tell you about yourself. Come out and try it.'

'Certainly not! I had better things to do even when I was a schoolboy.'

'You dirty little bugger!' responded Malcolm with a laugh that came from the subculture of the pub rather than from his persona as organizer of a self-seeking weekend. 'Ivor, you come out and have a go. Peter won't hit you. He just wants to demonstrate the scoring strokes to those who've never done it before.'

'Scoring strokes!' sneered the commander. 'You must think

148

we're bloody mad. Ivor! Where are you going?' Ivor walked awkwardly towards the centre of the circle, peeling off his jacket. He did not look as if he would give Peter much trouble. As Kelvin had once said, Ivor needed to stick matches in his ears before he had a bath to stop himself slipping down the plug hole. 'I fenced for Cirencester.'

'Oh, did you?' said Peter. 'Well, this isn't fencing. Stand there and I'll show you the scoring strokes.' He showed the scoring strokes: an upward stab to the base of the throat and the heart with a downward lunge into the bowels and the groin. Lesser strokes were incapacitating slashes at the joints.

'Pick up a sword and let's try,' said Peter. Ivor carefully selected the smallest sword, being closest to the *épée*, and flexed his wrist experimentally. Although he looked an inferior species of animal to Conan the Barbarian, many years of tugging the foremilk out of cows a couple of times a day had

preserved the strength and suppleness of his wrist and so he appeared quite professional as he took his guard and parried the first mighty swipe from Peter. It was the last mighty swipe. Ivor looked like a Disney cartoon character tottering away from an upswinging garden rake. The vibration from the parry and the sting in his fingers caused his sword to drop from a numbed hand and he stood there hugging his palm in his armpit as Peter, chanting 'One and Two', smacked him smartly on the knee and poked him in the belly, before standing back to admire his prone figure.

'See?' said Peter, turning his back on Ivor. 'It's very easy. Everyone pick up a sword and let's see you all work up an appetite.' The orchard rang like a bodger's battlefield as grown men circled, slashing at each other with their wooden swords, uttering squeals of apprehension and aggression.

The commander threaded his way through the mob to Ivor who was sitting on the grass, nursing his knee. 'You are a silly bugger! At your age, you ought to know better. Oh, hullo, Keith.'

Keith had only just arrived. He looked dreadful: gaunt, covered in bramble scratches, burrs and goosegrass, with a six-inch barbed-wire slash across the knee of his trousers. 'What's going on?' he asked, looking round at the battle.

'They're stripping away the dross of civilization,' replied the commander.

'They're all bloody mad. They must be as knackered as I am! What's up with you, Ivor?'

'That prat Peter thumped him,' replied the commander. 'Why don't you go and sort him out?'

'I think I might just do that. I've had about as much as I can take from this lot.'

Keith picked up Ivor's sword and plunged through the mob towards Peter. The latter was toying with a small, bald man who had his back to a tree and a terrified expression on his face as he defended himself desperately from the attacking blade as it crashed into the trunk, inches from his genitals. Keith had obviously summed up the chivalrous spirit in which the battle was being fought as he crossed the grass. With a

150

great 'Huzza' he jabbed the point of his sword into Peter's backside just as tears of humiliation were springing up in the eyes of his victim.

It may have been the effect of launching his attack on the run, or his judgement may have been affected by his lack of sleep, for even Ivor forgot his wounded knee to draw in breath with a hiss of horror as Keith slammed in his weapon. The effect on Peter was immediate: he screamed in agony, dropped his sword, clutched at his buttocks and rolled on the ground.

Combat gradually ceased as cavaliers, pirates, musketeers and Scarlet Pimpernels – even the odd samurai, specializing in a two-handed style – had their fantasies interrupted by the shrieks. They formed a grimly curious circle round him, resting on the hilts of their swords like Crusaders, satiated after a bit of good rape and pillage.

Keith was more into violence as a countryman than he had been in his days as a pork butcher in Reading; even so, he was appalled at the effect of his blow. 'Christ! I'm sorry,' he stammered. 'Are you OK?'

'Of course he's not OK,' said the commander. 'You jabbed him on the coccyx. It really wasn't the most honourable way to attack.'

'Bloody effective, though,' admired a spectator.

'You stupid bloody shit!' gasped Peter.

'I've said I'm sorry,' said Keith helplessly. 'There's not a great deal more that I can do.'

'Cows don't make half as much fuss when you break their tails,' said Ivor, who had wasted no time in hobbling over to appreciate the drama. 'Oh, it's all too easy to do,' he continued, responding to a couple of raised urban eyebrows. 'If you want them to go forward, you push their tails up above their backs and you have to be very careful or the bone snaps.'

'I am not a fucking cow,' moaned Peter. 'Although I think something may have broken.'

The commander inspected Peter as he writhed on the ground. 'Hmm. You do look a bit pale, but I should think you're probably just bruised. However, we could always ram a splint up if you really think something's broken.' Ivor and the commander exchanged a contented smile. 'They do say that sticks and stones may hurt your bones,' he continued remorselessly. 'I knew it would be dangerous to play with those swords. Let this be a lesson to you.'

'Go away,' groaned Peter. 'Please, all of you. I want to be alone.'

'That's Garbo,' said Keith.

'What is?' asked Ivor.

' "I want to be alone." '

'But she didn't get a wooden sword up her arse, did she?'

'Malcolm, take them all away!' pleaded Peter.

'You mean we've finished playing with the swords?' asked the commander.

'Yes,' said Malcolm briskly. 'What about some breakfast? After that, and when Peter's licked his wounds, we can go on to something else.'

'Breakfast! Now that sounds like a good idea, but I'm not sure I'd recommend that Peter licks his wounds,' said the commander. 'Or whether we should abandon an injured member of the party.' His protestation of concern would have carried more weight if he, Ivor and Keith had not immediately turned their backs on Peter and headed rapidly through the orchard towards the barn. The rest of the party, shepherded by Malcolm, followed, leaving Peter to find out what kind of man he might be when it came to coping with pain.

Chapter Ten

BREAKFAST DID little to convince the commander that he had made a wise decision in coming on the weekend. Keith seemed to be quite enjoying himself, while Ivor's way of avoiding involvement was through constant complaints. 'Call this food? I wouldn't feed it to my pigs!'

'You can't expect miracles when you feed twenty people off one camping stove and small campfire. I think we're lucky to get beans as well as half-raw bacon,' replied Keith.

Malcolm had at least chosen a reasonable place to make camp. The lichen-covered grey stone barn had been part of a farm whose house had long been demolished, although the outbuildings were still in use. Behind it lay the orchard and to its front was a stretch of grass-covered hard ground which had been the old yard, from where a lane led back alongside a stream to the public road. Beyond the orchard and on the other side of the river, the fields rolled up to the moor with tiny thistledown sheep dotted across the grass and heather. They were sitting on a fallen sycamore, a decent distance upwind of the fire which was fuelled by a sackful of artificial logs smelling as if they had been marinated in sump oil. Ivor had his leg carefully stretched in front of him to favour his injured knee. 'Do you know what we're supposed to be doing after this?'

'More cowboys and Indians, I should imagine. They've got shields and bows and arrows in the back of one of the Land Rovers.' The commander stared morosely at the majority group by the fire, hungrily watching some frozen sausages that remained obstinately willy-pink in the frying pan above the fake logs. He wrinkled his lip as he tasted the tea that had been sploshed into a tin mug for him. 'It amazes me. You can eat food on a destroyer that has been cooked during a force twelve gale and wouldn't shame an adulterer's bistro in Soho, while this is one of the worst meals I have ever experienced. How do you mess up baked beans, for instance?'

'It's not difficult when you try to poach them,' responded Ivor. 'Oh look! Here comes Peter. He must be feeling better.'

Peter was walking delicately back from the orchard towards the campfire. He moved like Robert Mitchum, as if there had been a slight interruption in communication between the upper and lower halves of his body, but he still managed a charming smile as he came over to the tree stump in response to the commander's beckoning arm.

'Feeling a bit better?' asked Ivor solicitously.

'Yes, thank you.'

'Good. I'd be a bit careful over breakfast if I were you.'

The commander looked puzzled. So did Peter. 'What do you mean?'

'The beans.'

'The beans?'

'Yes. In your condition you don't want any sudden shocks or explosions.'

'Is that why you wanted to talk to me?' asked Peter bitterly.

'No. I want to know what we're doing today – and don't give me any of that mystical secrecy bullshit.'

'Just walking.'

'Just walking?'

'Well, just about. It's a race between each group to capture a hill fort at the head of the river. Malcolm and I will defend it and there'll be a debriefing session there this afternoon at four.'

The commander raised an interrogative eyebrow. 'Is that all? No nasty little googlies that you'll tell us about afterwards?'

'No.'

'No?'

'No. Each group will be armed, of course.'

'Ah! Armed! Bags I the machine guns. Ivor and I can shout "Rat-tat-tat" and the other groups can fall down.'

'Your group has been allocated quarterstaffs. Each group can attack any other group it comes across en route.'

The commander rose to his feet and felt the seat of his trousers. He sighed. 'Well, dear boy. You can do what you like, but I am rather tired, rather dirty, rather fed up and I have now got a wet arse. I am going home. Are you coming, Ivor?'

'Yes.'

'How about you, Keith?'

Keith gnawed his moustache. 'I'd like to, Commander. But I said to Mandy that I'd be out until tomorrow evening and, you know, I wouldn't like to put her out.'

'My dear chap,' replied the commander, 'I quite understand. Elfrieda has gone off to a conference of Women in Socialism. So you'd be very welcome to spend the night with me.'

'You can't all go home!' said Peter. 'You'll change the spiritual balance of the weekend.'

'Tough!' remarked the commander.

'Well, you can bloody well walk home. I can't spare a Land Rover.'

'So be it. It's only a few miles and I suspect we'd walk us a damn sight further if we stayed.'

'You're afraid of getting hurt,' sneered Peter.

'Damn right I am,' answered the commander with some spirit. 'I could end up like you, walking around as if I'd been rogered by half the Home Fleet.'

'You're chicken!'

'Cluck cluck!' agreed the commander. 'Being wounded for one's country is one thing but it's quite another to be damaged in some Noddy weekend like this.' He picked up the haversack which contained his whisky. 'Ivor, Keith, we might as well get going. If we're quick, we'll be back for opening time.'

As the conversation had become more heated, so their voices had carried to the group by the fire who had come up to add their support to Peter's point of view. 'Huh!' snorted

155

Hugh. 'It didn't take you very long to discover what sort of a bloke you are.'

'I knew already,' replied the commander. 'Excuse me.' The crowd parted to allow the trio of deserters to pass through its midst.

Malcolm's was the only face that did not wear an expression of contempt. He caught up with them fifteen yards from the rest of the party. 'I'm sorry about this,' he said rather awkwardly. 'I shouldn't have pressured you into the weekend.'

'It doesn't really matter,' answered Ivor. 'It was our own fault for coming along.'

'Malcolm!' called Peter accusingly.

Malcolm looked back irresolutely. Ivor patted him on the shoulder. 'Get back to your playmates. I think it's in everyone's interest that we don't say too much about this back in the village.'

Malcolm looked relieved. 'I think you're right. Anyway, have a nice walk back and I'll see you next week some time.' He returned to the group as the commander and the other two ambled off along the side of the river.

They did not make it by opening time. The commander's brief look at the map had shown only half a dozen miles between home and their breakfast site, but they were not crows and the moors went up and down a bit. Some of the ups were very up and some of the downs, had they been alpine ski-slopes, would have been marked by black warning flags.

The crest of the third significant up they had tackled within a couple of hours was marked by an Ordnance Survey cairn and Ivor sat gratefully down in its lee to wait for the other two who were toiling below him, their hands grasping at the roots of the heather and bracken as they sweated their way up the hill. The commander was first to join him, followed closely by Keith. They lay beside each other, breathing heavily.

'You should have looked more closely at the map,' gasped Keith.

'I know,' admitted the commander. 'But it's too late to choose another route now. I should think we've still got two or three hours to go.'

156

'I think it's time we lightened our load,' suggested Ivor. 'Let's have a wee sensation.'

'A what?' asked Keith.

'Whisky.'

'Did someone mention whisky?' said the cairn against which they were leaning.

Keith and the commander were too exhausted to react but Ivor jumped for all three of them. 'Christ! Who said that?'

'It was the cairn, I think,' replied the commander. 'Judging by its accent, it's an American cairn. However, there is a possibility that it wasn't the cairn at all, but merely somebody round the other side of it. Ah!'

The 'Ah!' was the exclamation of a man whose theory had stood the rigours of experiment as the speaker entered his field of vision. The latter was an American, which was obvious from his uniform and the fact that the stripes on his sleeve were upside down. 'Have you guys got whisky?'

'Yes,' said the commander.

'Would you be interested in a trade for a bottle of Myers?'

'Myers?' queried Ivor.

'Rum, begod!' exclaimed the commander. 'That's what I would consider an interesting trade. Have you got much rum?'

'A dozen quarts.'

'How quaint,' murmured Ivor, who now thought in litres like a good dairy farmer.

'A dozen quarts!' exulted the commander. He raised himself up on his elbow and looked at the new arrival. 'If you don't mind me asking, what is an American serviceman doing hiding behind a cairn in this God-forsaken spot?'

'It's not that bad,' argued Ivor.

'It depends on your point of view,' replied the commander. His point of view had been forged by a twenty-minute hike up the side of a steep hill. However, when he cast a jaundiced eye, he had to admit that it was picturesque. They were on the edge of a marshy plateau that stretched across the barren heart of the moor. The heather rolled down to the sea a dozen miles away in one direction and to the misty summits of

157

the next range of hills across miles of fertile farmland in the other.

'We're here because of Operation Bulldog. It's an exercise to test NATO defences.'

'Ah yes!' said Ivor. 'That's the thing that Kelvin was so excited about. But what has that got to do with sitting on top of a hill with a dozen quarts?'

'We're a radio unit.'

When nothing else was forthcoming, Ivor looked at the commander who tapped the side of his nose. 'Oh, I see. We could be Russians.'

'You can never be too careful in a foreign country,' said American. 'My name's Willard. Come and meet the boys.'

They levered themselves to their feet and walked round the low tumulus in front of which the survey mark had been placed. There was a neatly camouflage-painted hut sitting incongruously behind it. 'How on earth did that thing get here?' asked Ivor. 'There isn't a road for three miles.'

The American caught their dumbfounded expressions. 'Chuck brought it in under a chopper yesterday.' He opened the door to reveal a couple of colleagues sitting in front of a bottle-gas heater. They were holding glasses and staring gloomily at a couple of pornographic magazines on the table in front of them. They turned as the door opened. 'We've got some visitors, boys,' said Willard. 'They got some whisky.'

'They got any women?' asked one.

'No women.'

'Shit! What are they doing here? Are they Red Force?'

'Are you?' Willard asked the commander.

'No. We're just going home.'

'Lucky bastards! Find something to sit on and have a drink.'

They had a drink and then another. They were all fast friends a couple of hours and a couple of quarts later. 'But what are you actually doing here, Billy Joe?' asked Keith, putting his arm round Billy Joe's shoulders.

'It's about as crazy as what you're doing here, Keithie baby.'

158

'Shit, Billy Joe,' interrupted Willard. 'We're supposed to be top secret. Tippity-top secret.'

'Who are these guys going to tell?' replied Billy Joe, flinging his arms wide in an expansive gesture, almost knocking Keith off the camp chair that had been provided for him. 'The fucking sheep?'

Keith put his hand on his heart. 'I promise we won't tell the fucking sheep.'

'See?' said Billy Joe to Willard. 'I told you these guys were OK. Anyone can end up playing cowboys and Indians with a bunch of jerks. It's not their fault.' He leaned confidentially across the table. 'We're here to guide in the attack this afternoon.'

'What sort of attack?' asked Keith somewhat nervously.

'Wheee!' said Billy Joe, skimming a rather shaky hand over the table top. 'We've got the whole US airforce coming along to bomb some goddam hilltop. We're here to tell them where to go. Wheee!' His speeding hand knocked the commander's glass and spilled a few drops. 'Sorry.'

'It's quite all right,' replied the commander. 'But surely they know where to go before they take off?'

'Half of the guys who fly those things don't know their right from their left.'

'Yeah,' agreed Willard. 'If it wasn't for us, they'd probably bomb London by mistake.'

'They don't use real bombs, do they?' asked Keith.

'Hell, no!'

'In that case, would it be all right if we stay to watch when they come over? It might be quite fun.'

'Hadn't we better be thinking about getting on our way?' protested Ivor.

'No, we're OK,' replied the commander, glancing at his watch. 'I think we could get to Frank Mattock's farm in an hour and he could run us into the village.' He emptied one of the rum bottles into his glass. 'Tell me, Willard, how low do the planes go when they make their bombing runs? What exactly goes on?'

'Depends. We've got one bunch in F111s and they take a

pride in taking the tops off molehills. We've got them and some Tornadoes this afternoon and they'll come in one by one in separate waves to zap the target. Wheee! It's quite a sight when they come in.'

'Hmm,' said the commander thoughtfully. 'And where is it exactly that they are supposed to be going today? And what time are they due?'

'The target is some hill or other over there.' Willard waved his hand vaguely westwards. 'They ought to be here at teatime.' He nudged Ivor who was sitting beside him. 'Hear that? Teatime! I can talk Limey real good!'

'Hmm,' said the commander once more.

'Hmm,' agreed Ivor. 'If you're thinking what I'm thinking, it's a jolly interesting idea.'

'What are you thinking?' asked Keith.

The commander poured Willard another whisky from their diminishing supply and leaned forward confidentially. 'How exactly do you guide them in?'

'On the radio. They're supposed to have a map reference. We watch them go by as well and if they're going the wrong way, we give them directions. What's all this about?'

'It occurred to me that it might be possible to change the reference.'

'Gee! I don't know about that. Hey! Billy Joe!'

Billy Joe had gone out of the hut to urinate and was declaiming from the top of the cairn that the wigwam of Nokomis stood by the shore of Gitchee Gumee. He broke off. 'Yeah? Whaddya want?'

'You got the reference for this afternoon?'

'No.' He returned to *Hiawatha*.

'Hell, I must have it then.' Willard shuffled his fingers though his pockets, pulling out a crumpled envelope. 'Here it is!'

'I'm glad about that. Can you change it?'

Willard looked dubious. 'I can do if there's an emergency. But I ain't needed to yet. It's supposed to be in sight so's I can report that they really wasted the enemy.'

'If you need an excuse, you could say the hunt were in the

160

area of the original target and you didn't want to frighten the horses.'

'The hunt? You mean lots of guys in fancy red coats? That would be neat! They'd love to send that to the Pentagon as a reason for a change of target zone. But what's the point of changing the target?'

'Yes, what's all this about?' asked Keith plaintively.

The commander smiled. 'Peter is holding his hill fort against warriors with swords and bows and arrows. It would be rather nice to call in an air strike against him.'

Keith gave a long sigh and sagged back in his canvas chair. 'Ohhh! That's beautiful!' He turned to the American, his moustache wiffling with yearning. 'Please, Willard.'

Willard rubbed his chin thoughtfully. 'I don't see why not. It would sure spoil your guy's day. What's the target like?'

'Let's have a look at the map.' The commander pulled a dog-eared tourist map of the moor from his pocket and traced back the stream to its source. 'There! That must be it. There's only one hill fort in the area.'

'Let's see that,' demanded Willard. 'Hey! Look at the contour lines! It must stand up like a pimple on a hooker's ass at the top of that valley. Yeah, that looks fine. The only snag is that we won't actually be able to see the strike from here.'

The commander studied the map, spread on the table in front of him. 'That's true. But if we go over there, we ought to have a good view. We can tell you how well they . . . er . . . did their zapping.' He indicated the edge of the plateau on the paper. About a mile west of the hut, the ground dropped steeply into the valley.

Willard traced his finger over the map. 'It should be perfect. The aircraft'll make their run up the river and hit that castle place at the top. Is it a real castle like they have in Disneyland?'

'No, it's just a mound with a few rocks on top. It's prehistoric.'

'Shame! It'd be great for the flyboys to bomb a real castle.'

'It's just practice, remember,' said Keith.

The Americans had to stay in the hut with their radio, but

161

the other three left later in the afternoon, allowing twenty minutes for a gentle stroll across to their vantage point. There was a convenient scattering of boulders on which they placed cushions lent for the occasion by their American friends. The commander brought out a flask: 'I didn't want to waste this before. It's a single malt which is really rather fine.' He had a neat little stack of silver cups in a leather case and he carefully filled them and handed them round. He placed his own cup carefully on his boulder, took his binoculars – also borrowed from their hosts – and put them to his eyes. He scanned the valley up to the hill fort which was half a mile away. He gave a grunt of satisfaction. 'Ah! I can see them. There are a few figures actually on the top and there's others milling round below it. They look as if they're playing tag.'

'They're probably having their war,' said Ivor contentedly.

'It's really very pretty up here,' observed Keith looking round at the view. 'It's a shame that Mandy and I don't come up to the moor more often.'

'It's not really Mandy's sort of thing, is it?' suggested the commander. 'At least, not with you. Me, perhaps, but not you.'

'I suppose you're right,' agreed Keith wistfully.

The commander looked at his watch. 'They should be coming over any second.' He held up his hand. 'Hark!' They hearkened. There was a sound of distant thunder. 'Timing's not bad. Although I suppose it's only a few minutes in one of those things from East Anglia or wherever it is they live.'

'There!' pointed Keith. Its wings swept back, a slim jet skimmed up the valley below them. Beneath the greeny-brown camouflaged wings, the points of four missiles were visible. The thunder of its engines cracked the air as it raised its nose to skim the ramparts of the mound before climbing towards the sinking sun. 'By God! That's a sight and a half! That must be one of the F111s they were talking about!' The end of his feverish comment was drowned by the next aircraft, the vibration of whose passing seemed to resonate in their bowels as it streaked over the top of the hillock.

The commander put the binoculars back to his eyes.

'They're all flat on their faces!' he shouted. 'Even the ones at
the bottom of the hill!'

Keith jumped up and down with excitement as jet after jet
screamed up the valley. As the last echo of the last plane
rumbled into silence, he turned to the others, his eyes shining.
'To think we did that! I've never known anything like it! I'd
love to be able to do it again!' He gave a sudden shriek of
delight as the whisper of approaching engines suddenly
became a roar. 'The Tornadoes! I forgot the Tornadoes!' The
Tornadoes were smaller and stubbier than their predecessors,
but more than adequate for their task. Through the binoculars,
the commander could see tiny figures running away from the
fort as the first aircraft of this second attack crashed through
the air just above their heads, then another and another, their
huge noise almost having a life of its own divorced from the
tiny planes.

The valley returned to silence once more save for the
shocked crowing of a cock pheasant in a wood a couple of
hundred feet below them. Keith sat back on his rock, groped
for his silver cup and downed its contents in one gulp. 'That's

163

the finest thing I've ever seen!' His lips were quivering with emotion.

The commander shot him a quizzical look round the binoculars. 'Steady on, old chap! I hope neither Reagan nor Gorbachev thinks the same as you.' He scrutinized the scene below. 'However, I think it can be safely said that we won today's battle. Gentlemen, shall we return our binoculars and go home?'

'Shall we tell Malcolm that we were responsible?' asked Keith.

"Oh no,' said Ivor.' I think it would be much nicer if we didn't. Let's keep it a secret.'

Kelvin laughed so much when he told Malcolm on Monday evening that his false teeth fell on the floor of the pub and broke.

Chapter Eleven

'I THINK IT'S a disgrace,' said Stephanie Jarrett firmly, sinking her teeth into one of Mrs Baggins's rock buns. Like her husband, Stephanie was an intellectual, so the other women paused in their conversations to listen. Women's Institute meetings had changed in character quite recently. They used to be highly traditional, serving the needs of the older women in the parish – lots of competitions for the best jams, the prettiest teatowels, and lectures from members about visiting the Tower of London while their husbands were getting drunk at the Smithfield Show.

Then it changed, thanks to the local newspaper. It had always carried reports of the area's WI meetings under the heading 'Ladies' Groups'. A fresh editor had cast a critical eye at the grey columns of funerals, auction reports and the lists of those done for possession of cannabis or non-possession of television licences and decided to liven it up a bit. In the first editorial in living memory he had announced his improvements. In the classified advertising section motors were moved from after property to before, and the column which included WI reports was no longer headed 'Ladies' Groups' but 'Women's Groups'.

The shifting of 'Cars for Sale' had no discernible impact upon the community, but the other change did. A Women's Group was a very different animal from a Ladies' Group and light-years away from the Ladies' Circle to which the yuppier spouses of the Round Table members belonged so that they would have a chance to wear expensive evening dresses at their annual dinner-dances where they gyrated the night away to the accompaniment of pina coladas and a trio of middle-aged men in gold lamé who sang *Yesterday*, *My Way* and *Viva L'España* to remind them of their summer holidays.

The term Women's Group had serious overtones. It conjured up topics like abortion, feminism and muesli-flavoured, hand-woven, recycled lavatory paper, and this attracted fresh members to the WI, including Stephanie Jarrett who had a sociology degree and Elfrieda who was not only against nuclear weapons but had actually been to Greenham Common. It was rumoured that the commander now had to iron his own shirts.

'What's a disgrace?' asked Mrs Baggins nervously. She was afraid that it might be her rock cake to which Stephanie was referring.

'That we seem so inward-looking in this community.'

The subject under discussion was 'Charity begins at home', not quite as potentially explosive as 'Lesbianism as a political issue' which was promised for the following meeting. This was already the subject of caucuses amongst the older members about what it meant and what they could possibly contribute to it.

'For example,' continued Stephanie, 'I heard Dennis say that he had refused to put anything in the plate when the collection in church was going to African refugees because he thought that we ought to take care of our own first.'

'Well, he may be right,' replied Mandy, one of the stalwarts of the old WI who was rather enjoying the new look. Mrs Baggins still hankered nostalgically for the days when she won a contest for putting the greatest number of objects inside a matchbox.

'I doubt it,' argued Stephanie. 'But that's not what I object to. It's the fact that so many people round about say things like that and then do nothing for any charity closer to home.'

'Marcia gives a buffet lunch at the manor for the World Wildlife Fund every year,' said Mandy.

'That's not quite the same as giving to the starving in the Third World and, anyway, most people only go to the manor for social rather than charitable reasons.'

'I think you're being unfair,' contributed Lindy.

'Well, just ask around. Find out how much people know and how much they give and to what.'

The pub was interested in what went on at WI meetings. Just as it had been awed by the number of things that Mrs Baggins had managed to stuff into her matchbox, even though it was a Swan Vesta box, so it mulled over Stephanie's accusation. In essence, it was true that people did look inward, but not because of heartlessness. They did not feel themselves part of the international community. Even those in a village half a dozen miles away were considered to be foreigners, while anything that appeared on television or in the national press might as well have taken place on Mars. The state of the greenfly on the roses in front of the pub was of much greater interest than what went on at arms control talks in Geneva.

However true it was, nobody liked to admit it. 'I think we're very generous in this village,' said Bill. 'Remember in the spring when the school wanted some gym equipment? The kids did a sponsored spelling test and they raised nearly £100.'

'Yes, that's quite right,' agreed Ivor. 'And the village hall fund grows year by year.'

'Look at the jar on the bar,' said Keith. They looked at the large glass sweet jar crammed full of pennies which were given to the Guide Dogs for the Blind every Christmas. It made them all feel a little better.

'I think that proves Stephanie's point,' said Helga from behind the bar. 'She is just saying that people here only give when it's close to home. Giving for gym equipment and to the village hall is just giving to ourselves.'

'But you can't say the same about that jar,' responded Keith.

Helga looked at it. 'You can hardly suggest that the odd penny from your change for a pint of beer is a great charitable sacrifice.'

'It's not just the odd penny!' exclaimed Kelvin who was peering in through the side of the jar. 'See that silvery bit?' They all followed his pointing finger. 'That's got to be the edge of a 20p piece.'

167

Keith picked up the jar, with some difficulty, to give it a shake and make sure that there really was a piece of cupro-nickel in there. The glint of silver disappeared in a sea of pennies. 'I can't see it,' he complained.

'Well, it was there all right. That's what I call really generous. I wonder who put it in there? It wasn't me, was it, Helga?' Kelvin asked anxiously.

'Don't be silly,' scoffed Ivor. 'You'd never put in 20p.'

'If I hadn't got my glasses on and if it was fairly late in the evening I might. Anyway, it must have been one of the customers and it proves my point that we're a generous lot here.'

'It was put there by a rep from one of the brewers,' said Helga tartly. 'I once saw Frank Mattock give 2p, otherwise nobody has given more than a penny. You've never put in anything, Kelvin.'

'Thank Christ for that!' exclaimed Kelvin with relief.

'You ought to be ashamed of yourself, Kelvin,' said the commander who, up until then, had been holding his peace.

'Why?' demanded the latter indignantly.

'Your attitude. I knew a seaman who raised £500 for Oxfam when he was only eighteen by getting sponsored for walking to John O'Groats. It may have been Land's End, but it was certainly somewhere like that.'

'Silly bugger!' muttered Kelvin under his breath.

'£500! I could really admire a man who could do that,' said Helga. She was a spectacularly beautiful woman, somewhere in her forties with a glamorous 'Mittel European' background who had somehow come to take over the pub. Business had boomed when it was realized that she was not interested in converting the place to a tourist's gin palace and was prepared to allow gumboots into the public bar. She had every male in the village licking her hand and wishing they had the opportunity to lick more interesting portions of her anatomy. She exploited this devotion shamelessly, making one man strive against another to achieve her favours and, since she was a thoroughly nice woman, her influence in the community was wholly beneficial – as, initially, in this instance.

168

'Admire a man who could raise £500?' asked Kelvin.

'Oh yes! It would show that he had a beautiful soul if he'd do that for other people.'

There was a short pause. 'I could raise that easy, if I wanted to,' said Kelvin.

'It wouldn't be that hard, I'd've thought,' agreed Ivor and the other men present murmured that they were of the same mind.

'You're all wonderful!' breathed Helga, who had learned that she had to lay it on with a trowel during the year or two she had been in the pub. She winked at Stephanie who picked up the baton.

'That's easy for you lot to say, because you're all talk and no action,' she said. 'When it comes to doing anything practical, you're all hopeless.'

'I'm not all talk!' said Kelvin.

'Right then,' said Stephanie briskly. 'You'll raise £500 in sponsorship for Oxfam.'

'I didn't say I'd do that,' replied Kelvin evasively.

'Kelvin!' cried Helga. 'You wouldn't let me down.'

'Well, no,' he agreed miserably.

'Excellent!' cried Stephanie. 'And the rest of you will do something as well?' Grudging although it may have been, there was definite assent.

'But what will we do?' asked Ivor. 'We can't do a sponsored spelling. Some of us would never get any money.' The locals were experts at deciding the worth of a bullock or the tonnage of grass on a field, but 'readin'n'ritin' were not their strong points. 'Rithmetic' was different as it was needed to count up money.

'That's true,' agreed Kelvin. Literacy was a clerkish talent and slightly effeminate.

'I'll organize one of the things that the teenagers at school do when they're sponsored.' Stephanie taught at the comprehensive school in the nearby town.

'All right, you do that. But make sure it doesn't need too much learning,' said Kelvin.

'Or too much exercise,' added Bill.

'Right,' said Stephanine. 'I'll have something worked out by lunchtime on Sunday.'

After church on Sunday was an important social occasion in the pub. Very few would have actually gone to church but more would dress up in their Sunday best to visit their local hostelry.

The publican had always put out free peanuts and crisps and Helga enriched the event by adding sausages on sticks and canapés.

Stephanie and Malcolm Jarrett turned up with Napoleon, the pimply teenage son of Mandy and Keith. He began to stuff sausages into his mouth with grim concentration, annoying other customers who would have liked to do the same if it were not for the fact that age had made them self-conscious.

Conversation flowed easily. The men had almost forgotten about their money-raising pledges and the suggestion that a new drain should be put in the gutter outside the post office was by far the most relevant topic of the moment. It had been tossed around in the parish council for several months from where it had recently emerged to be debated in public. Stephanie waited her moment. She decided that it had come when Kelvin snapped at Napoleon after he had finished off the sausages and was moving into the solitary bowl of cashew nuts.

'By the way,' she said casually. 'I brought along Napoleon because he was sponsored for £50 last year.'

Napoleon managed to smile proudly and chew at the same time. The commander had bought him a pint of orange juice to force him to fill his mouth with something other than cashews, but he was using it to wash them down, thus increasing his speed of intake.

'For eating large amounts, I suppose,' commented Ivor with some distaste.

'No, nothing like that. I thought he was jolly brave.'

'So did I,' agreed Helga. She presented Napoleon with a warm smile. It was wasted on him as he was picking his teeth, but noted enviously by everyone else.

170

'I'll do the same and I bet I get double the money,' said Kelvin stoutly.

'If you're man enough,' smiled Helga.

'Man enough to do what he can do?' questioned Kelvin incredulously, nodding towards Napoleon. The latter was at the gangly stage and his fashionable drainpipe jeans accentuated his general air of weediness.

'Anything he can do, I can do better,' hummed Helga.

'You'd better be careful what you get yourself into, Dad,' warned Prudence. The stolid fruit of Kelvin's loins was rarely seen and even more rarely heard. She came to the pub on Sunday with her father but had rarely been observed to do more than belch discreetly after a couple of glasses of mild ale.

Kelvin had obviously not expected advice from that quarter either. Startled, he looked at her. 'What's with you, then, Missy? Do you not think your old father knows what he's doing? There's nothing he can teach me. 'Course I'll do what he's done.' He turned to the other male regulars. 'We all will, won't we?'

With a combination of Kelvin's crude stick and Helga's seductive carrot, all agreed.

'You are all wonderful!' said Helga. 'And the money you raise will go to help the world's hungry?'

'If you think that's the best place for it, then that's where it will go. I'll show you what generosity is. Commander, if you sponsor me, I'll make sure that Prudence sponsors you.'

'That sounds a fair enough offer,' agreed the commander. 'But what exactly did you do, Napoleon?'

Napoleon chewed, swilled, swallowed and answered. 'I went round and got everyone to fill in my form and they paid up afterwards.'

'Yes, I know that, but what did they sponsor you to do?'

'A parachute jump.'

There was complete silence in the room, broken only by Jimmy pawing at the commander's arm. 'What did he say?' he asked plaintively.

'Jesus Christ!' replied the commander shortly.

Jimmy considered for a few seconds, before turning to

171

Helga across the bar. 'I don't understand. What does he mean by that?'

'It's all right, Jimmy,' replied Helga. 'He said parachute jumping.'

Jimmy looked annoyed. 'Well, why did he say "Jesus Christ", then?'

'Think about it,' answered Helga. Jimmy thought about it and began to shake. A wheezy laugh, not unlike the death rattle of a donkey, escaped from him, driving the smoke from the hand-rolled cigarette, which was permanently attached to his bottom lip, towards the commander in a series of rancid puffs.

Jimmy was seeing the bright side of having a gammy leg, emphysema and being into his seventies.

Those who would be unable to claim medical exemption were still absorbing the implications and were startled by Prudence opening her mouth. 'A parachute jump! Oh, I've always wanted to try a parachute jump. Can I be sponsored as well, Stephanie?'

'Of course. All these men have volunteered but, as you're the first woman, I'll put £1 down myself.'

Kelvin was aghast. 'Prudence! What's wrong with you? A parachute jump! You're off your bloody head!'

'You're going to do one too,' replied Prudence.

'I'm bloody not. If you think I'm jumping out of a sodding aeroplane, you're insane.'

Helga knew that she had to employ every aspect of her genius. 'Kelvin, you promised!' she said reproachfully, a little sigh, as delicately sensual as the zephyr from a hummingbird's wing as it sipped nectar from the blossom of a hibiscus, escaping between the warm gules of her lips. Of the imperatives that drove Kelvin, lust came after cowardice, gluttony, vanity, avarice, envy, malice, sloth and a host of others. She realized that she was being too subtle and so leaned over the bar to display her cleavage and placed a soft hand on his grey-stubbled cheek, tracing a finger down to the point of his jaw. 'Kelvin, I'd be so disappointed.' He wavered slightly and she pressed her advantage home. 'How would you

172

like a drink on the house?' She was assaulting on several fronts. Lust, avarice, gluttony and vanity were all under attack. The other men looked on in concern. With Kelvin crumbling, what possible chance would they have?

'Mum's going to have a go. It's easy, if you've got the bottle,' sprayed Napoleon through a shrapnel-shower of roast ox-flavoured crisps.

'Mandy? Is Mandy doing a parachute jump?' asked the commander incredulously.

'That's right,' smiled Stephanie. 'She's bought a yellow jumpsuit for the event.'

All the men, save Kelvin, looked worriedly at each other. He was looking down the front of Helga's blouse as she pulled him a pint.

'I'm not sure that this is a particularly good idea,' remarked Ivor. 'It's a young person's game, you know. We chaps are not as physically resilient as we used to be.'

'There's no need to worry. We had a grandmother in her seventies doing a jump for the school last year.'

'It takes a bit of bottle,' swaggered Napoleon. 'Fatty Hutchings who's in our class said that she felt really scared when she stepped out of the door of the aircraft. She's just a kid, though. She was really scared of *Driller Killer*.'

The bottomless pit that was before the patrons of the pub yawned wider and wider with every word spoken. Stephanie carefully gave them the little push. 'I've sent an announcement to the local paper about it and they will be sending along a photographer on the day.'

The commander sighed, knowing that he was trapped. 'When's it going to happen?'

'I thought in a couple of weeks. I'm told it's a quiet time for the farmers which means everyone will be able to make it.'

'Will you sponsor me, Helga?' asked Kelvin hoarsely.

'Of course, darling. I think you're wonderfully brave. I shall come along too. Napoleon and I can sponsor each other.'

That was it. There was no more that anyone could do about it. Ivor had the last word on the subject. He sank his pint and smacked it down on the bar. 'Oh shit!' he remarked crisply.

It was extremely naive to expect Kelvin to jump from an aeroplane. There was a bit of speculation when he failed to appear in the pub the following Thursday lunchtime, but it was put to rest that evening when he limped proudly through the door. His foot was in plaster. Bill looked at him and sighed.

'What's happened to your foot, Kelvin?' he asked resignedly.

'It was Ramrod. Bloody animal. It's really most annoying.'

Ramrod was his elderly, foul-tempered bull, mostly Friesian, which spent the best part of his time in a small shed that could have doubled as the Black Hole of Calcutta with the addition of a yard's depth of dung. The animal had the run of an adjacent pen where he performed his duties, but he preferred to stand inside his shed where he thought evil thoughts and rolled his eyes in fury at the sparrows which scavenged round his feet. With advancing years, Ramrod had grown casual about copulation and sometimes lay along the back of his spouse and daydreamed. In that instance, Kelvin would take a sprig from a convenient clump of nettles which grew beside the pen and tickle the animal's testicles. It had a galvanic effect but did nothing to add to the *tendresse* between master and beast.

'I suppose that means you can't jump,' continued Bill.

'I really don't know how I can,' Kelvin said, trying to look disappointed.

'What happened?' asked the commander, taking on the role of inquisitor.

'The bull stood on my foot.'

'I see. And why is it in plaster?'

Kelvin looked at the commander. 'It's broken, you bloody fool. Why else do you think it would be in plaster?'

'Let's just get this quite clear. The bull stood on your foot and broke it. What exactly were you doing at the time?'

'Standing behind the bull, of course. I was whipping its arse with some nettles and it stepped back.'

The commander did not know the fine print of Kelvin's relationship with Ramrod but he had trodden inadvertently on too many spectacularly bizarre examples of local mores

174

and behaviour to wish to know more. After a brief pause, he moved hurriedly on with his line of enquiry. 'And where was Prudence when this happened?'

'Prudence? I dunno. I think she was helping out with dipping sheep next door.'

'I see,' said the commander. 'What happened then?'

'I went to hospital and had it plastered up, of course.'

'Ah!' said the commander triumphantly. 'And how did you get to hospital?'

'In my van—'

'—But how did you drive with a broken foot?'

'Very, very carefully,' replied Kelvin without hesitation. He had had a lifetime of bluff and counterbluff in the hard school of agricultural dealing and there was no possibility that an innocent like the commander could catch him out. 'I really am very disappointed. I was looking forward to the experience and, of course, raising lots of money for Stephanie's darkies.'

'How long will it be before the plaster comes off?' asked Helga.

'Why?' asked Kelvin suspiciously.

'Just wondering.'

'Hmm.' Kelvin thought for a few seconds before replying. There was no obvious benefit to him in not giving the right answer to Helga's question and this worried him. If people told the truth in response to a question, you would never know what to believe. Vagueness was safe. 'It depends how it gets on. I shouldn't think it'll be on for more than a few weeks.'

'I was just thinking that there's no reason why you shouldn't enjoy a jump of your own when you're better.'

The inhabitants of the bar looked at Helga as if she was mad. Even Kelvin. It was just possible that Kelvin had really broken his foot and, if he had, it was just possible that it had happened fortuitously. Much more likely was that the foot was intact under its white covering or that Kelvin had been attempting a bruise that had got out of hand. Whatever had happened, he was certainly not going to waste such an excuse.

Kelvin laboured unsmilingly on. 'Even when the plaster comes off, there'll be no telling how long it will take for the

175

foot to get back to normal. In fact, at my age, it may never be
quite right and it could well break down again when I'm least
expecting it.' That was almost enough, but you never knew
with Helga. 'I'm quite sure that my medical advisor would
never allow me to parachute again.'

'Again?' queried Ivor with a disdainful curl to his lip.

Kelvin turned his attention to Ivor with relish. 'But you can
be quite sure that I won't miss the jump. I'll be along to give
all the help that I can. I can imagine what that moment when
you step out into thin air might be like. The howling of the
wind and the hard ground rushing up to meet your body. It
can't be all that much fun. After all, even Fatty Hutchings was
quite concerned about it.'

'You bastard!' said Ivor, turning rather pale.

'It's a cruel, cruel world,' said Kelvin cheerfully.

Chapter Twelve

THOSE WHO had agreed to jump had lived long enough to understand that the future, however dreaded, was bound to become the present at its appointed time, and so there was phlegmatic acceptance in the air when the day finally dawned. Even Kelvin, who gave the commander and Ivor a lift in his van to the airfield, could not generate much fear in them on the journey, although he did his best.

'It's a good thing I'm bringing the van along,' he had ventured into a strained silence. The silence was actually due to a deep concern about the quality of Kelvin's driving which was being felt by his two passengers. 'I said, it's a good thing I'm taking the van,' he repeated rather more loudly.

'What?' asked the commander. He had his hands on the dashboard and both feet braced against the floor. They were not braced as hard as he would have liked as, due to the condition of the vehicle, they were quite likely to pass through into thin air.

Kelvin, under the impression that he was bemused with terror at the prospect before him, turned to the commander to savour the emotion. The van was not travelling fast but, with Kelvin's vague supervision totally withdrawn, it lurched drunkenly across the narrow lane to ricochet off the opposite hedgebank. 'Damn!' muttered the driver, spinning the wheel to bring it back on course.

The commander cleared his throat. 'Kelvin, if you kill us before we get there, you'll spoil your chance of seeing us killed when we make our jump.'

Kelvin looked shocked. 'I don't want to see anybody get

killed. I just want to see you all thinking you might be killed. A bit of suffering, that's all. Mind you,' he continued musingly, 'I do owe Ivor £65 and I wouldn't have to pay if he didn't make it. Saving £65 would go a long way towards helping me to cope with my distress.'

'I'd have thought 10p would be a big help. For £65 I'd expect you to've done the job yourself,' said Ivor caustically.

'That would be against the law!' stated Kelvin disapprovingly. There was a pause while they all calculated the distance between the van and a rabbit which darted out of the hedgerow across their path. Kelvin fought to regain control of the van after he had swerved towards it. 'I'm glad I brought the van along,' he repeated doggedly.

'I'm not,' moaned Ivor from the back.

'I'm glad I brought the van along because it can double as an ambulance on the way back.' There was silence. 'Or as a hearse,' Kelvin added hopefully. He kept trying, but his passengers refused to rise. The van turned out on to the main road, cutting across a stream of traffic and rattling up to 50mph for the last few miles towards the airfield. He was feeling rather depressed when they arrived.

Even the commander, who had crunched down on to the decks of aircraft carriers in his time, looked askance at the limp windsock dangling over the molehill-scattered length of grass and the rickety barn which was, apparently, the hangar. 'I hope their planes all have MoT certificates,' Ivor remarked nervously. 'I mean, it's not exactly Heathrow.'

'We won't be up there for long and there's no need to worry about the landing,' comforted the commander, eliciting a snort of laughter from Kelvin who rather wished he had thought of that line first. The van bounced across the grass to pull up alongside the other cars already parked by the barn and its passengers emerged to follow the sound of concerned voices which were coming from the building's interior.

The hangar seemed to have been converted from a small warehouse which, in its turn, had incorporated the original barn at one end. There was only one aircraft at which they were all staring with alarm. It was clear what the problem

178

was. It was a small and extremely tatty biplane about twenty-
five feet long, painted a faded green. It was a two-seater with
one seat set behind the other and both open to the sky.

'Good grief!' said Ivor. 'That thing looks lethal. I'm not
going up in something like that.' He turned to Napoleon, who
had come along to give people the benefit of his expertise. 'I
thought one was supposed to have static lines and things like
that. Are we expected to climb out on to the wing like some
bloody circus act and dive off? I think it is quite outrageous
that we should be called upon to go up in that. I vote we go
home.'

That was the best idea that anyone had had for weeks and
his suggestion was hastily endorsed. It took Kelvin, standing
in the doorway of the barn and flapping his arms as if to divert
a stampeding herd of cattle, to prevent them rushing back into
their cars, twittering with relief at their narrow escape from a
thoroughly nasty experience, and driving off home. 'Stop!' he
thundered just before the retreat became a rout. 'Friends!

179

What is wrong? Where is your pride? Think of those more unfortunate than yourselves who stand to benefit this morning from your activities. Can you let those . . . er . . . kiddies down?'

'Kelvin, for heaven's sake! Would you fly in that thing?' demanded Ivor as he tried to sidle round the outstretched arms.

'Of course! If only I could. Nothing would give me greater pleasure. If I had not hurt my foot, I'd be up there like a shot.' He emphasized his determination that this should have been so by stamping his plaster-covered foot noisily on the ground. 'But I can't.'

'In that case, mind your own business,' said Mandy tartly. 'And get out of the damn way!'

'There's got to be a mistake, Kelvin,' contributed Napoleon. 'There's no way that this lot can be expected to climb out of that thing and jump.'

'Mr Morchard to you, sonny!' snapped Kelvin. 'And children should be seen and not heard.'

'Ah! But out of the mouths of very babes and sucklings hast thou ordained strength,' Napoleon surprisingly replied.

Kelvin was spared the need to cap Napoleon by the arrival of another car, its body a delicate filigree of rust. The driver of the wreck emerged and retraced the path of his vehicle, tidily picking up pieces of it that had become detached when it had taken to the grass. He was a bald, painfully thin man in his forties with a concave chest, a great beak of a nose jutting from his face on which was perched a pair of thick-lensed spectacles, and he wore a jumpsuit rather like Mandy's, although his was blue and faded rather than yellow and new.

'What the hell's that?' asked Kelvin.

'That's Budgie. He's a nuclear scientist,' said Napoleon.

'He doesn't look as if he's been eating his Trill!'

Budgie had collected a sidelight amongst other things, and put them into the boot of his car. He slammed down the lid and came over to the barn. The boot slyly re-opened behind him. 'Hullo,' he said, surveying the scene. 'You're a pretty funny-looking lot,' he remarked.

180

'You're a bit of a joke yourself, mate,' responded Kelvin reasonably.

Budgie looked at Kelvin and then at his plastered foot. For a man who seemed as if he must have had sand kicked in his face for much of his life, he showed few signs of being downtrodden. 'I don't know what the hell you've come here for. You're not going up with a foot like that.'

'Are you something to do with this business?' asked the commander.

'If by "business" you mean the jump, the answer is yes. I'm the jump master.'

'Are you now?' remarked the commander grimly. 'In that case I should inform you that we have decided that none of us are going up.' He looked defiantly at Budgie.

Budgie shrugged. 'Suit yourself.'

'Don't you care?'

'Why the hell should I? You're the people who wanted to jump.' He turned back towards his car. 'I'm off home, then.'

'Don't you want to know why we won't go up?' asked the commander, rather miffed that so little interest was being shown in such a momentous decision.

Budgie, already beginning to walk back to his car, stopped and turned back. 'Not particularly. Quite a lot of people turn chicken when it comes to it. It's no skin off my nose.'

'That's a relief,' muttered Dennis to Helga, thinking about the amount of skin that might come off a nose the size of Budgie's.

The commander ploughed doggedly on. 'It's nothing to do with being chicken, as you put it. Only a lunatic would risk their lives in a set-up like this.'

Budgie smiled. 'Look, I don't need to hear any excuses. I quite understand. It's nothing to be ashamed of, although I'd rather you'd decided to back out earlier so that I could've done something more profitable with my day. I only came because Stephanie said that quite a lot of money would be raised.'

The commander turned rather red. 'I don't think you've quite got the point. It's nothing to do with us being scared.

181

It's just that everything here looks *contrapted*.' Everyone nodded agreement. Budgie's car suddenly let the air out of one of its tyres, sagging even closer towards the tarmac with the gusty sigh of relief of a fat man subsiding on to a toilet seat.

'Oh bugger!' said Budgie. 'The spare went last night.'

'That's just the sort of thing we're afraid of,' said the commander, grateful to the car for choosing such a well-timed moment to provide him with evidence to buttress his case.

'What the hell are you talking about?' asked Budgie, dragging his eyes back from the car to the commander with irritation.

'If your bloody car behaves like that, what the hell is that wreck of an aeroplane in there going to do?' He indicated the machine squatting in the background with a jerk of the thumb.

Budgie looked at him with scorn. 'Don't pretend you thought we'd use the Gypsy Moth there. It's being restored – it hasn't even got an engine in it.'

'Oh,' said the commander, uncertainly.

'There's a nice spanking new plane flying in here this afternoon,' continued Budgie. He smiled, 'Look, I really don't mind. Nobody's forcing you to go up.'

Ivor spoke up. 'You mean we'd be parachuting from a decent aeroplane?'

'Of course. And the parachutes are virtually new and they're all checked twice.'

The change in attitudes was magic. Kelvin's desperation and depression lifted from his head like a cloud and sailed across the intervening few yards to settle on the commander, Ivor and Dennis. Even Mandy, who had been coming to an unpleasant understanding that her new jumpsuit carried with it certain responsibilities, was finding the silver lining rather hard to spot.

'That's all very well,' the commander blustered, 'but you can't expect us to hang about here all morning, waiting for some chum of yours who might fly by later on this afternoon.'

'You tell him,' agreed Mandy.

'You won't be hanging about,' smiled Budgie grimly. 'You've all got to be taught how to fall – like this.' Budgie suddenly crumpled at the knees and did a complicated little shimmy which resulted in a somersault, his feet slapping down in a patch of mud which splashed Mandy's jumpsuit. He got up, brushed himself down and smiled once more at the commander. 'You'll enjoy that, won't you?'

'Jolly impressive,' agreed the commander, gnawing nervously at the tip of his moustache.

'Has anyone got a tissue?' asked Mandy. Prudence rootled around the pockets of her nylon milking overall and passed over an udder cloth which Mandy pointedly used to rub the mud carefully into her suit. It was an extremely colourful garment, light yellow at the crotch with the hue gradually darkening as it spread out to her extremities. It was rather like one of those paintings by de la Tour, lit by a single candle. 'I don't see why we have to do that sort of thing,' she continued. 'It looks awfully undignified.'

'I can assure you that it's a lot more undignified if you break your leg on landing,' said Budgie.

'Or your neck,' added Kelvin, beginning to get back into the swing of things.

'Is it decided, then, that we're going to do this jump?' asked Dennis gloomily.

'I'm afraid so,' confirmed Ivor.

'I feel like the bloke in the electric chair who has just been told of his reprieve when the prison governor comes rushing in shouting "April Fool!" '

'Right! Quiet please!' ordered Budgie. 'We've got a lot to get through before you make your jump.' His audience looked at him in trepidation. 'You!' he pointed at Kelvin who jumped, unused to being addressed by a man accustomed to command, particularly one who looked as unimposing as Budgie.

'Me?' he asked.

'Yes. Go to my car and you'll find some parachute harnesses on the back seat. Rig them up on that frame.' He indicated a horizontal iron bar about ten feet long, supported

183

on a couple of wooden posts six feet high in one corner of the shed.

'Why do I have to do it?' complained Kelvin.

'Because I'm not having you hanging around all day like a priest in a whorehouse. If you're going to be here, you might as well make yourself useful. When you've done that, you can start brewing up some tea. You'll find a stove and everything else in the back.' He turned. 'Everyone else, please sit down on those benches over there and we'll get started.' Budgie strode over to a blackboard propped up against the wall and began to draw diagrams.

'He's got a bloody cheek!' spluttered Kelvin. 'I've a damn good mind to tell him who I am. Just because he is daft enough to jump out of aeroplanes, he thinks he can order folk around.' Grumbling, but softly so that Budgie would not hear him, he limped pointedly out of the shed and towards the car.

Budgie may not have been everyone's idea of an intrepid sky diver, but he was good enough for Prudence, particularly as she had never seen her father do as he was bidden with quite so little fuss. There were stars in her muddy brown eyes and her spectacular bosom rose and fell rapidly within the confines of her milking overall. 'I like him,' she announced as everyone seated themselves on the benches. 'But why should he think that Father was like a priest?'

'In a whorehouse, dear, no use to anyone,' replied Mandy.

'Oh, I see.' Prudence thought for a moment and emitted a great guffaw of laughter. 'He's very witty, too.'

'Very witty,' agreed the commander. 'I bet he's a barrel of laughs when he chucks people out of the aeroplane.'

'You!' said Budgie, turning from the board to point at the commander. 'Pay attention unless you want to end up as a smear on the runway.'

'Barrel of laughs,' agreed Dennis, under the cover of another guffaw from Prudence, earning her a thin smile from Budgie which made her blush.

Stephanie arrived in the middle of the day, bearing a large hamper. The problem of lunch had been interfering with the

184

concentration of Budgie's bench-bound audience who abandoned him in mid-sentence and descended on the hamper. It contained pasties, sausage rolls, home-made cakes and bottles of parsnip wine, for which Stephanie had a growing reputation in the community.

Budgie gracefully accepted the pasty and glass of wine brought to him by Prudence and, at her request, launched into a dissertation on quarks and neutrinos as she sat at his feet, her mind flicking between the charming way that he tugged at his hair when he became excited and the difficulties he would face in adapting to life as a farmer's spouse after they were married, particularly with a father-in-law such as his would be.

Budgie broke off as Dennis and the commander glumly came over to join them. Dennis was clutching a whisky and the commander was braving the parsnip wine, but neither of them was hungry. 'Looking forward to this afternoon?' asked Budgie.

'At least we'll soon have it over with,' replied the commander.

Budgie bit deep into his pasty and chewed carefully as Prudence picked up his scattered crumbs from the concrete floor with a dampened finger tip and popped them into her mouth. Budgie opened his mouth. 'Jerfth fthhusth,' he said, spraying bits of pastry from between his lips. Prudence looked at them and decided to leave them where they lay.

'I beg your pardon?' asked Dennis, fishing a small piece of chewed potato from his whisky.

Budgie swallowed. 'There's a German lad coming in this afternoon to join us for the landing training. He's been badgering me to teach him to jump for weeks so I asked him to join us. He's flying in with Charles on the Cessna.'

'German?' queried the commander, wrinkling his nose.

'Charles?' asked Prudence.

'Cessna?' added Dennis, just so that he would not be left out.

They waited patiently for answers as Budgie chewed his way through another bite of pasty. For such a skinny human

185

being, he had evolved a remarkable capacity for packing large amounts of food into his mouth at one time.

'Yes,' he said eventually, before taking another large bite.

'What do you mean "yes"?' asked the commander, irritated.

'Prffly phthls,' replied Budgie.

Dennis appraised him thoughtfully. 'If we asked him questions, he could tap the floor with his foot. One tap for yes and two taps for no.'

'Splutthus,' said Budgie. He made an attempt to swallow and turned red in the face.

'I'd say he's bitten off more than he can chew,' contributed the commander.

At this point Prudence retreated, moving along the floor on her bottom so that she was out of range of all but the largest lumps that were propelled from Budgie's lips.

Dennis looked inquiringly at Budige. 'Who's Cessna?' he asked. Budgie stopped struggling to close his mouth and succeeded in conveying disgust through his eyes and a wrinkle of his nose.

'You are a fool, Dennis,' admonished the commander. 'A Cessna is an aeroplane, isn't it, Budgie?'

Budgie nodded vigorously, swallowed convulsively and, before anyone could prevent him, stuffed the remaining third of the pasty into his mouth.

The commander sighed. 'Charles – is he the pilot?' Budgie nodded. 'And this German. Is he all right?' Budgie shrugged. 'Is he like Helga?' Budgie gave the commander a strange look.

Dennis helpfully interpreted. 'He would look extremely odd if he was like Helga.' Budgie nodded appreciatively.

'I didn't mean physically like Helga. I wanted to know whether he had been in this country for a long time or whether he was still quite . . . er . . . German.'

'You're not prejudiced against Germans, are you?' asked Dennis loudly.

The commander cast a worried look across at Helga to ensure she was not within earshot. 'No, of course not. But some of them can take life a little too seriously.'

'We're not throwing a party, so I wouldn't have thought it'd matter if he was a bit po-faced.'

Just then the sound of an aircraft was heard and they all went to the door of the hangar to watch the Cessna come buzzing over the tops of the trees, to land on the grass strip of the runway. It lurched across the bumps and potholes towards the small patch of concrete that had been laid in front of the hangar.

'I wonder what the pilot will be like?' mused Prudence, beginning to have second thoughts about Budgie as a life partner as she picked a few crumbs from her hair.

'It's a very small aeroplane and the runway looks very bumpy,' said Mandy, with the experience of a couple of flights between Palma and Luton to draw on.

'I'm sure everything will be all right,' reassured the commander. 'Budgie knows what he is doing.' He glanced back at the jump master who was still munching away in the hangar. From somewhere he had dug out a doughnut and had artificial cream smeared all over his face. The commander cleared his throat nervously and returned his attention to the aeroplane which, with a final flourish of the engines, rocked to a halt in front of the hangar where its two occupants emerged. The pilot was slim, cavalry-twilled, thirty-five, cravated and wrapped in sunglasses. His passenger was in his late twenties, well over six feet tall, with blond hair, broad shoulders and wearing a dazzling white pair of overalls. The sun emerged from behind a cloud as he climbed out and stretched. He gleamed.

'He looks like an angel!' exclaimed Prudence.

'More like a recruiting poster for the *Luftwaffe*,' the commander replied sourly.

'Good afternoon,' said Dennis as the pilot walked delicately up to the group.

'God, I feel awful. I'll never do that again,' he replied.

'Do what?' asked Mandy.

'Fly with a hangover like I've got at the moment. Booze and coke really aren't the best thing the night before flying. I didn't think I'd be able to make it. Has anyone got some aspirin?'

'I've got some in my handbag,' said Mandy.

'I implore you to bring me a handful!' Although he was in shadow and wearing sunglasses, he still shaded his eyes with his hand to look at her. 'Better still,' he continued. 'I'll come inside with you and have a little lie-down until you want to start leaping about the sky.' He tottered into the darkness of the hangar. Then he stopped and turned, nodding towards his passenger who was now bouncing across towards them, his golden curls forming a nimbus round his head: 'Make sure you keep that prick away from me!'

Dennis watched him give Budgie a wide berth and lie down on an old sofa behind the biplane. 'Oh dear, oh dear, oh dear,' he sighed. 'The more I get into today, the less I like it. It was bad enough when we just had to face a parachute jump, but it never occurred to me that we'd be putting ourselves in the hands of Laurel and Hardy.'

'What's so bad about mixing booze and coke?' asked Mandy. 'I love it with rum.'

'It's all right if you're drinking it. I suspect that Charles was probably sniffing it,' replied Helga.

'Really? What an odd thing to do! He's lucky he didn't drown himself.' Mandy gave the beautiful German a dazzling smile as he reached the hangar.

He smiled back. 'The top of the day to you. I am Helmut Krause. I am going to be a parachutist because I am strong and brave. Are you old persons here to be looking at me?'

'Jesus wept!' exclaimed the commander with horror. 'He's one of them!'

Helmut Krause looked stiffly at the commander. 'I would be knowing you that I like womens. I am well appreciated for my loving of ladies' bottoms. You are most uncourteous to say that I am men's man. I strike at dishonourers!' Helmut raised his fist in a symbolic striking.

'Mad, too!' gasped the commander, missing the symbolic nature of the gesture and skipping behind Prudence for safety.

'Nutty as a pumpernickel. God preserve us! Helga, can't you reason with him in his own language?'

'I don't speak German. I am from Rumania.'

'Really?' said Dennis with interest. 'I had always thought you were German or Austrian.'

Prudence was now face to face with Helmut. He may have fulfilled the commander's criteria for insanity, but she had lived with Kelvin all her life and hers were less rigid. Prudence knew cattle, not people, and Helmut, unlike Budgie, would have made a prince among bulls – excellent conformation, the probability of a good conversion rate and, by his own admission, an interest in the craft of procreation without which a bull is merely beef. She was not quite certain about how to indicate that her milking-overall-clad posterior was a bottom for the loving, but she thrust it out anyway, jarring the startled commander back a pace.

The movement drew Helmut's attention to Prudence and her relevant portion. 'You are not old like the others. Are you to be watching me?' he asked.

Prudence looked puzzled so Mandy, miffed at being considered old like the others, helped her out. 'I think he wants to know if you're here to watch him jump, not just to look at his beauty.' She sniffed. 'I don't know who the hell he thinks he is. He obviously keeps his brains in his biceps and his balls, unlike the commander.'

'Helmut Krause, pretty woman.'

'Well, Helmut Krause. We are all here to make a parachute jump. All except Kelvin over there.'

'You josh with me,' replied Helmut incredulously. 'It is young men who are strong and brave like me who do this thing. Old bones will break like dry sticks when they hit the ground. I know bones. I am a chiropractor.'

'Dry sticks!' quavered the commander, his imagination shuddering. 'Budgie!' he wailed. 'Could you come here a minute?'

Budgie had by now done his eating and was on to his teeth-picking. He ambled over, his middle finger working away on a wisdom tooth. He gurgled interrogatively.

189

'Budgie, do we have to do our jump with Helmut? I'm sure he's very nice and everything, but he's going to have a dreadful effect on morale. Tell him to go away, please. I think I speak for all of us?' The commander looked at everyone else. 'Except Prudence.'

'I told you the man was a prick.' Charles's voice came from the shadows of the biplane. 'I wouldn't mind a drinking coke, by the way, if anyone has got one.'

Kelvin, who had been avoiding being given any further work by skulking in his van with a copy of *Farmers' Weekly*, sensed some drama and appeared in the hangar doorway.

Budgie took his finger from his mouth. It glistened. 'What's wrong with Helmut? He looks a clean young man.'

'He's saying that we'll all end up with broken legs, for a start.'

'Not all of you,' Budgie demurred, eliciting a gleeful snort from Kelvin who could not have put it better himself.

'For heaven's sake—' the commander started, but he was interrupted by the voice of Charles.

'Don't worry, old son. You'll be all right. Budgie's only joking.'

'Are you?' asked the commander.

Budgie answered with an enigmatic smile. 'It's time you were taught the practical side of the business. Will you all please go outside on to the grass.'

Helmut did all that had been expected of him during the two hours' training. When he fell, his rolls were impeccable, bouncing immediately back to his feet without touching the ground with his hands, to sneer at his fellow fallers who would still be thrashing about on the grass. He counted the seconds between the simulated leaving of the aircraft and the simulated pulling of the ripcord on the emergency parachute so loudly that Charles, still recuperating inside the hangar, yelled at him to shut up as his booming voice was setting up sympathetic resonance in the corrugated iron of the building's walls. When he actually simulated the pulling of the simulated ripcord of the emergency chute, he cried in a mighty voice and smote Dennis, who was practising more diffidently beside

190

him, smartly in the pit of the stomach.

By three o'clock, Budgie decided that his pupils were as ready as they were ever going to be. He divided them into groups of four for their first leap. The first batch consisted of the commander, Mandy, Helmut and Prudence, who were chivvied into the belly of the aircraft where they squatted on the floor, the bulk of their parachutes precluding them from taking their places on the seats. With an expression of grave disquiet on his face the commander looked through the gap in the side of the fuselage, from which Budgie and Kelvin had taken the door, at those who were due on the next drop. Mandy was more concerned that her harness was too tight. Prudence, who had been waggling her bottom at Helmut like an unco-ordinated wagtail for much of the day, was still looking appreciatively at him as he raised his arm to the onlookers with the craggy confidence of Kirk Douglas saluting to the crowd before starting combat in the Colosseum.

The noise of the engine was loud inside the aircraft, but not loud enough to drown out Helmut who, with shining eyes, was declaiming like an Old Testament prophet in praise of himself rather than the Lord. 'Ha! You will see. I will fly like a bird. I shall roll correctly when the ground strikes my feet, but I shall land so gently that I still can stand. See me, people: no virgin in a parachute shall do it like me!'

'The mind boggles,' said the commander drily. Having someone like Helmut around certainly took his mind off speculating why Budgie suddenly uncrossed his fingers and regained colour in his cheeks as the aeroplane hopped, skipped and finally jumped uncertainly into the sky, the ground disappearing from view at alarming speed.

'Yes!' cried Helmut. 'I shall boggle too as I fall like – how do you say? – like a star which flies through the sky seen by Halley. Like a comic! Yes, I shall fly like a comic!'

'Oh, for Christ's sake, shut up, you fool!' snapped Mandy. 'Wait until you are out of the aeroplane and then you can babble away as much as you like.'

'You are frightened, yes?' asked Helmut with Kelvin-like sympathy. 'Have no fear. I shall show you the way.'

Ten minutes after take-off, Budgie stood up. Holding carefully on to the roof of the aircraft, he walked the couple of steps through to the cockpit and had a quick word with the pilot before coming back.

'Right!' he shouted. 'Who's first?'

Helmut sprang to his feet. 'I!'

'—Said the fly,' added the commander.

'*Nein*, the comic,' said Helmut.

Budgie clipped the static line on the back of Helmut's parachute to the ring bolt on the roof and clapped him on the shoulder as he climbed gingerly through the doorway. The style of exit had been carefully explained and even more carefully listened to. Left hand on the edge of the doorway, left foot on the step that was attached to the aircraft just below the doorway, then a lurch outwards so that the right hand could clutch the strut below the wing while the remaining limb was left to dangle in space. This left the body spreadeagled alongside ready for a yell from Budgie at which one let go and followed one's line of sight to the ground beneath.

Helmut carefully climbed out of the plane, his crash helmet the same snowy white as his overalls. The commander shut his eyes as his stomach began squat-thrusts in protest at the risks it would shortly undergo through no fault of its own.

'Go!' yelled Budgie, leaning out to smack Helmut on the arm.

There was a hoarse cry above the roar of wind and Budgie stepped back, turning towards Prudence. 'Are you next?' he shouted.

'Yes,' said Prudence, struggling to her feet.

The commander tapped Budgie on the knee and indicated the hole in the fuselage. Helmut, his face contorted in a rictus of fear, was clinging with both hand to the base of the doorway, trying to haul himself back into the cabin.

'I said "Go!" ' yelled Budgie.

"I am not an insane. It is too far long down.'

The commander was surprised to find that he had instinctively clutched Mandy who was sitting beside him. She

had clutched back and he glanced sideways to find his own expression of appalled terror reflected in her face. Helmut heaved himself up in the doorway.

'I said "Go", you yellow bastard!' Budgie put his boot on the centre of Helmut's chest and pushed. The commander and Mandy watched helplessly as Helmut was whisked out of sight by the slipstream. Budgie leaned out for a few seconds to follow his progress before he pulled himself back. 'Right. Next!' Prudence moved across to the doorway, her expression revealing neither apprehension nor disappointment at the craven behaviour of her intended. The commander briefly reflected that courage may have been a quality to be bred for in the bulls of Andalucia, but Prudence would be seeking one who was tractable and docile. Budgie clipped her line to the bolt and she stepped out of the aircraft as if she were stepping out of a bus. 'Go!' yelled Budgie, and she went.

Budgie turned, his eyes raking the rest of his prey. 'You!' He indicated Mandy. 'Come on!'

'Fuck off!' replied Mandy, holding tightly on to the commander's hand. 'If you think I'm moving from this floor, you must be mad.'

'All right,' said Budgie mildly. 'Nobody's forcing you.'

'You mean you're not going to throw me out?' asked Mandy.

'Of course not. I am not a barbarian. The other chap was out of the aircraft and he had to go. But you can do what you like.'

'Oh,' replied Mandy, rather deflated.

Budgie turned to the commander, raising an interrogative eyebrow. The commander considered. Short of being locked in a small room with Kelvin for eternity, there was nothing that he could think of that could fill him with greater apprehension than the concept of jumping out of the aircraft. On the other hand, there was his reputation and honour to consider, not to mention those who would benefit from his sponsors' money. If Prudence could do it, so could he, and the idea of showing himself a better person than Helmut was almost irresistible. It was Budgie who tipped the scales by removing the word 'almost'.

'One thing's certain,' he shouted in the commander's ear. 'It'll be a damn sight safer to jump out rather than risk landing with Charles in the state he is.'

The commander rose to his feet feeling like Sidney Carton on his way to doing a far, far better thing, and Budgie clipped on his line. He stepped to the hole in the fuselage and leaned out to grasp the strut. His hand missed and he overbalanced to somersault out of the aircraft. 'Hell!' he said to himself phlegmatically, as he tumbled through the air, thinking vaguely that he ought to be counting, pulling ripcords and doing all the other things that Budgie had been drumming into him. However, he was much more interested in wondering why he was not seeing his whole life flash in front of his eyes before he hit the ground. He was doing his best to help by trying to recall his earliest memory when he felt a jerk and looked up in surprise to see a parachute canopy sailing serenely in the air above his head. He looked round at the scenery below as the sound of the aircraft's engine faded into silence and decided to start enjoying himself.

Back on the ground, the spectators watched the parachutes drift down. Prudence landed on the edge of the runway and stood up immediately to begin rolling up her parachute as she had been taught. Helmut touched fairly near the hangar and, true to his prediction, he landed on his feet with hardly a flex of the knee. He was shouting before he hit the ground: 'It was magnificent! I fly like a comic or a hawk!' He gathered his parachute to his bosom and walked over to his audience. 'Did you not think I was like a comic?'

'Oh yes,' agreed Dennis. 'You were like a leaping young lion or a hart panting for the pool.'

'Like a hart. That is good. You are fortunate that you will soon be in the sky.'

Prudence had come over and was standing by. Dennis turned to her: 'What was it like?'

''S'alright, I suppose. The commander might be in a bit of a

195

pickle, though.' The commander had drifted over the edge of the airfield and had landed amid a herd of heifers. One might have thought that the animals would be used to curious aerial happenings in the field next door but they had seized the opportunity to charge round and round the field with their tails in the air while the commander lay prone beside his collapsed parachute.

'He's killed himself!' exclaimed Kelvin, rushing towards his van and starting it up. Dennis dived into the passenger seat and, with Helmut hanging on to the running board, they bounced across the field towards the fence.

'What's that noise?' asked Kelvin as they cleared the edge of the runway.

Dennis looked out of the van window. 'It's the plane. I can't think what the pilot's playing at. He was just above us. Oh dear, I think you may have driven across the runway when he was trying to land.'

'The silly bugger must have seen us and we had right of way. We were on the runway first.'

'I'm not sure that it works that way,' replied Dennis. They stopped by the fence. Helmut cleared the low barbed wire with an elegant bound. Kelvin, in spite of his gammy foot, was only just behind him, while Dennis was more circumspect and crawled through. The commander sat up as they approached and Kelvin's face crumpled with disappointment. Dennis felt that, if Kelvin had reached the commander in time, he might well have struck him with a stone to keep him down.

'What the hell's wrong with you?' demanded Kelvin. 'Lying around like that! We thought you had done yourself a nasty injury or something.'

'I winded myself. I quite thought I was dead for a bit and, when I found that I wasn't, I rather wished that I had been.' The commander sighed and rose shakily to his feet. 'Thank God that's over, anyway.'

'What happened to Mandy?' demanded Kelvin. 'Did her parachute fail to open or was she cut in half by the propeller?'

'I'm afraid it was nothing exciting like that. She just decided that she didn't want to jump.'

196

'That's shocking!' exclaimed Kelvin, who had come to the same decision a lot earlier.

Dennis and Helmut rolled up the commander's parachute for him while he watched the Cessna come in for its second, uncluttered, approach to the airstrip. 'It wasn't really her fault. After Helmut's performance, I can't say I felt much like jumping myself.'

'Helmut's performance?' asked Kelvin, eagerly. He was scrabbling a bit. He really wanted the dirt on one of the locals which he could embroider at great and scandalous length during the sunlit years of his retirement. With nothing else really juicy being fed to him, Helmut might have to do.

Helmut swiftly moved in with a pre-emptive shut-out. 'I fly like a bird, yes?' he said to the commander. 'I show clearly the great spirit of manhood?'

It was that questioning note in his voice that made Kelvin lick his lips. He looked eagerly at the commander. The latter sighed. He couldn't bring himself to do it. 'The great spirit of German manhood, certainly.'

Helmut stiffened, a war between national and personal pride ricocheting between the hemispheres of his brain. Personal won. 'Like a bird,' he said weakly. 'You too are a brave and gracious person.'

'How kind of you to say so,' gracioused the commander. 'Now, if you would carry my parachute to the van and hold the fence for me so that I can get through . . .'

Kelvin sniffed. There was something he had missed but he could not quite work out what.

Napoleon, Helga, Dennis and Ivor were Kelvin's last chance so he followed every move of the second trip, burrowing for uncertainties and weaknesses amongst the participants. He watched them select their parachutes with beady eyes, passed comments on the inadequacy of their crash helmets and pointed out Charles, sneaking a surreptitious few pulls on a bottle of vodka to steady his nerves after the last landing. But all agreed that a pissed pilot with his nerves intact was better than a shattered one with a hangover.

197

The light wind had died between the first and second flights and so those on the ground were able to watch four parachutes snap into existence above them as Budgie jettisoned his cargo. Kelvin sighed: at least last time only three had opened, leaving room for some delightful speculation.

Three thumped into the grass by the runway and regained their feet with varying degrees of grogginess. An errant breeze sighed gently up to the fourth, Dennis. Just when he was trying to recall whether he should roll left or right on landing, it stealthied beneath the parachute and puffed, imparting both lift and momentum.

Whereas Helmut had spun like a teetotum as he tugged his toggles in a frenzy of activity to prove that he had control, Dennis hung on the parachute straps like a sack of potatoes. Looking as unmoved by his fate as the corn before a combine, he drifted over the heads of the spectators and landed with a crash on the iron roof of the hangar. Kelvin was the first to react. It may not have been as exciting as a golden fireball at the end of the runway, but beggars could not be choosers. Ever an optimist, he rushed towards the hangar door, hoping to find Dennis neatly filleted, lying beneath a jagged and bloody hole. There was no sign of him, so Kelvin ran outside hoping to see him splattered across the roof.

The anarchic zephyr was not quite finished with the parachute. The silk bellied briefly once more, lifting off the roof across which it had been tastefully draped. It carried Dennis with it, rumbling him across the corrugated iron to the gutter and tumbled him the dozen feet to the ground.

The commander congratulated Kelvin on his forethought in bringing his van to act as an ambulance. Kelvin should have been delighted but he wasn't, since the patient stretched out in the back, as the commander rattled carefully through every pothole, was himself. Dennis had landed safely when he was blown off the roof, but only because Kelvin had been underneath his point of impact. Kelvin had a broken collarbone.

Within a week he was overheard telling a tourist in the pub

that he had sustained it while parachuting. It was only another couple of weeks before he was talking about what it felt like during his jump to the commander and Dennis. The pub pondered on the Nature of Truth. One Truth was that he did not jump; another was that he had persuaded himself that he had; and the third, the one that ultimately counted, was that he had carried his conviction round his cronies in the livestock market and made them stump up £300 in sponsorship. The last was the only Truth with a price tag, so, of course, it was accepted.

Chapter Thirteen

'BUT WHAT CAN I do about it?' demanded the commander. 'I thought I was getting somewhere up to that parachute jump, but now she's coming at me again like an express train.' The commander had endured an undeniably difficult few months since Mandy had decided that he was the one for her. 'It's not as if she's after me the whole time – in many ways I wish she was, because I'd at least know where I stood. But she can go for a day or two and be quite rude to me – just like normal – and then she'll come at me again like a randy tarantula. I tell you it's bloody terrifying. And with Christmas not all that far away, there'll be lots of parties and it'll be a misery.'

'It's a shame for you,' consoled Kelvin, who felt that he ought to react since the other two in the bar, Jimmy and Bill, were sitting slackly on their stools, enjoying that peaceful vacancy of mind in which the locals had the ability to pass hours at a time. A couple of months ago they would have listened with interest to the commander's complaints, but they had seen it happen for themselves, and a sight of the commander's terrified face when her 'Yoo hoo!' pierced through the hubbub of a social gathering told them more than his words.

'But what can I do?' the commander reiterated with despair. 'It's colouring my whole life. I almost dread coming in here because she might come in too. And I haven't been near the post office for a week. The last time I tried to go, she was standing in her doorway waving at me as soon she saw me!' He shuddered.

Kelvin looked blank. 'What's so awful about that?'

'She was wearing a pink nightdress that barely came to her knees!'

Kelvin was impressed. 'Heaven's above!'

'And that's not all. On her feet were a pair of those slippers – mules, I think they're called – and they were made out of white fur with a red pom-pom on the instep.'

'Heaven's above!' repeated Kelvin. 'And what did you do?'

'What else could I do? I turned and ran.'

Kelvin thought for a few seconds and sighed. 'I don't suppose there's much else you could do.'

'That's my point. Can't you think of anything?' the commander pleaded.

Kelvin considered. Initially he and the rest of the community had enjoyed the commander's understandable apprehension at being the object of Mandy's desires but it was now clearly beginning to wear the man down. That did not matter in itself, but it had turned him into a bit of a bore. 'You've become a bit of a bore,' said Kelvin.

'With that damned woman coming at me with the determination of a Mountie, do you bloody wonder?' cried the commander.

Bill turned his eyes towards the victim. 'Tell her to piss off.'

'Piss off? Tell Mandy to piss off? Even if I could tell a lady to piss off, just how do I go about it with Mandy?'

Bill looked nonplussed. 'Just open your mouth and tell her, of course.'

'Mandy?'

'I don't see why not. She's just another woman.'

Kelvin's sense of equity felt constrained to intercede. 'Be fair, Bill. You could hardly call Mandy "just another woman".'

'Quite!' acknowledged the commander curtly. 'In fact, there are precious few of the fair sex round here who could be so described.'

'Except Prudence.'

'With the possible exception of Prudence,' admitted the commander. He spun round as the door opened, but it was only Malcolm who came to the bar, rubbing his hands briskly together. 'Cold, this evening.'

'Winter drawers on,' said Kelvin as he had said a couple of times each autumn for the last forty years.

'What's fresh?' asked Malcolm, pouring himself a pint and putting the money in the till.

'The commander's moaning about Mandy again,' said Kelvin.

'Still? Why don't you tell her to piss off?'

'Jesus!' exclaimed the commander.

Malcolm had the grace to look contrite. 'Well, no, perhaps you couldn't do that. But you do seem to have been going on about it for some time. I'm amazed you don't do anything about it.'

The commander literally shook, like a man suffering from an ague. 'What? You stupid sod! Tell me what! It's all very well for you lot to tell me that I ought to be doing something, but none of you come up with any ideas!'

'You never asked me,' replied Malcolm huffily.

The commander turned wild eyes towards him. Life was quite clearly getting him down. 'You think you may be able to help?'

'Well, yes, I suppose so. It's merely a question of breaking down the problem into its constituent parts.'

'Like what?' demanded the commander eagerly.

'Well ... um ... let's think.' Malcolm paused. 'Mandy fancies you and you don't fancy Mandy. That seems to be the basis of it.'

'Yes. We know that. But how does that help?' asked the commander.

'It lets us know what we have to work on. Here we have two separate areas which might be changed. We can either try to make Mandy stop fancying you or else make you fancy Mandy.'

'It would be very convenient if we could make the commander fancy her,' said Kelvin. 'Remember, we wanted someone to take her on in the first place.'

'No! Certainly not! I don't want to fancy Mandy.'

Malcolm put a consoling hand on the commander's shoulder. 'There's nothing to worry about. If we make you fancy her, you'd want to.'

'But—'

'How could you make him fancy her if her doesn't?' asked Kelvin. 'Old Granny Chilcott had a line in love charms which she sold to the local maids so that they could snare their man. But I never heard that they did much good.'

'Commander,' said Malcolm patiently, 'just imagine for a second that Mandy really was the object of your desires.' The commander did his best, but his imagination was not up to it. Few imaginations would have been. Malcolm understood his difficulty. 'All right. Forget about Mandy. Who do you really fancy?'

Bill and Jimmy came out of their dark-brown studies to look curiously at the commander as he leafed through his mental catalogue. 'Well . . . er . . . your Stephanie comes to mind. She's a very fine-looking woman.'

Malcolm's eyebrows arched in surprise. 'She is? . . . . I mean, I know she is. Well . . . I suppose you'd better imagine that Mandy is Stephanie. No.' He broke off. 'Look, couldn't you think of someone else you fancy? It feels uncomfortable using my wife as an example.'

'Yes, I'm sorry. It just slipped out. I'll think of someone else.' His brow furrowed.

'Well?' demanded Malcolm after a few seconds.

'I'm sorry, I can't think of anyone else,' replied the commander sheepishly.

'There are probably 2,000 million women in the world. You can surely think of one to lust over apart from my wife.'

'It's that running shirt she goes around in,' apologized the commander. 'It really is rather impressive.'

'I know Keith admires her when she's out joggling. And so do I,' contributed Kelvin with relish.

'It's jogging,' said Malcolm worriedly. 'Keith? You've heard Keith talking about it?'

'By "joggling" I mean "joggling". I don't think Keith has tried it on, but he'd certainly like to.'

203

Malcolm took a deep breath. 'Commander, imagine that Mandy is not Mandy but Brigitte Bardot.'

'Right!' agreed the commander. He leant his arms on the bar to concentrate.

'We don't have a possessive relationship, but Stephanie wouldn't look at Keith. Surely not. No . . . the only time in the last few weeks when she went off by herself was that weekend and Keith was with us.'

'How long do I have to go on imagining Brigitte Bardot?' asked the commander, cocking an eye towards Malcolm.

'Oh, sorry . . . er . . . what was it I was trying to say?'

'I haven't the faintest idea.'

'Don't ask me,' said Bill in response to an inquiring look. 'I didn't understand a word of it.'

'Oh, bugger it. Let's try something else. If we can't make you fancy Mandy, we'll just have to make her stop fancying you.'

'That sounds much more the sort of thing I'm after. What do I do?'

'Be rude to her.'

'Look, I can't. Quite apart from getting my head bitten off, the poor woman's in love. One can't just rudely reject that. I imagine she's got human feelings like anyone else. I want her to reject me. That's the decent way to play it.'

Malcolm sighed. 'I admire your sensibilities, but you're asking for a great deal. Think what she feels when you jump through windows whenever she comes into a room. A quick clean break would be much kinder in the long run.'

'For heaven's sake! I've made it clear enough for any creature this side of a rhino! And she and I will probably be living in the same community for some time to come. I don't want to make a huge enemy of her.'

Malcolm held up his hand. 'OK. If that's the way you want it, you'll just have to make yourself sexually unattractive to her in some way, but retain her friendship.'

'That's it! That's exactly what I want! How?' The commander leaned forward eagerly.

'The best way is to turn gay.'

It was as if someone had sunk his fist into the commander's belly. He sagged back on his stool. 'Damn you! he said savagely. 'I thought you were going to come up with a sensible suggestion.'

'It is a sensible suggestion!' replied Malcolm indignantly. 'It may be a bit devious, but if you pretend to be gay, it's bound to change her attitude towards you. You go out to Julian's tomorrow and get some tips on how to act gay.'

'It's ridiculous!' scoffed the commander. 'Quite apart from anything else, I'm married and it's obvious that I'm . . . er . . . normal.'

'Oh, I don't know,' contributed Kelvin. 'Your Elfrieda is one of those Peace Women these days and you just have to see them on telly to realize that they're all a bit funny. It would be quite likely that you might be a homo because I've heard that two homos often get married. I'd find it quite believable if someone told me you were a homo.'

'How dare you!'

'Of course, you being in the navy helps too. Everyone knows what sailors are like.'

The commander, purple with indignation, cast around savagely for a crushing retort. 'You . . . you sheep shagger!'

Kelvin sucked in his breath in mock horror. 'That's a terrible thing to say!' He winked at Jimmy and Bill who were also enjoying the commander's discomfiture.

The commander noticed the wink and slid down from his stool. 'There are some things that are just not amusing,' he said curtly. 'I'm not staying around here to be insulted. I'm going home.' He nodded icily to Malcolm, ignored the others and walked over to the blackened oak settle by the fire to pick up his coat. The others watched him with interest since he had left a good half-pint of beer in his glass on the counter. He turned as he reached the door to cast another disdainful glance at the bar just as Kelvin was stretching out towards the glass in order to beat Jimmy to it. 'Here!' he shouted. 'That's my beer! Leave it alone!' He moved swiftly back to the bar, just as the pub door opened behind him.

'Yoo hoo, Commander!' His hand froze just as the glass

205

reached his lips. The heads of everyone else swivelled towards the door. Mandy loomed in the doorway in a high-neck angora sweater whose colour matched her red tweed skirt. She was also wearing red plastic boots with a pair of deeply dimpled knees bulging over the top.

'Ah! Mandy!' said the commander nervously. 'I'm just off. See? I've got my coat on.'

'Well, you can just take it off again, can't you?' replied Mandy gaily. 'Now I've got you, I'm not letting you go that easily! It's been days since we've had any time together. I've been beginning to wonder if you've been avoiding me!' She wagged her finger.

'Oh, no . . . er . . . well,' stuttered her victim.

'Grrr!' growled Mandy with a little pout. 'I could eat you up!'

Kelvin thumped the bar in his delight. 'That's it, Mandy! The bugger's really been lusting after you! You should hear what he's been saying.'

'For heaven's sake, Kelvin! Stop talking such tommy rot!' The commander's voice rose to a squeak as Mandy's hand sneaked beneath his coat and sharply nipped his bottom. 'Mandy! Control yourself! Stop it at once!' But Mandy merely laughed.

'Malcolm!' cried the commander despairingly, as her fingers encircled his wrist and she dragged him off to the far side of the settle by the fire. 'I'll do it! I'll do it!'

The hotel, which lay a couple of miles downstream of the village, gave the community a touch of class. It was an authentic Victorian fishing hotel, bulging with stuffed trout, brown Windsor soup and slumbering generals. The only note of incongruity was its proprietor, Julian, an outrageously camp London interior decorator, who had inherited the establishment from a bewhiskered aunt who had run it for thirty years. He had been there for four years and the hotel was thriving since the generals had all discovered that their wives became putty in the face of his flattery and preferred to hang around the hotel, hoping to be stroked by Julian, rather than follow them out to the river or demand to be taken round the National Trust properties within driving distance.

Julian was ambivalent about local custom. He liked the amount of money that the villagers could spend across his bar, but his elderly gentlefolk rubbed shoulders uneasily with Kelvin, Jimmy and their like. It was not a class conflict but little mannerisms that could give rise to complaints, such as the way Jimmy would cough up the tarry deposits from his lungs and shoot them accurately on to the toe of his boot, or Kelvin's habit of sipping from other people's drinks if their backs were turned. Nevertheless, he greeted the commander, Kelvin and Malcolm from behind the reception desk with a warm smile as they pushed through the heavy, mahogany front door and settled down to wipe their feet as he had taught them on the enormous coir doormat that guarded the entrance hall.

'Good evening, you lot. This is a rare honour. Is it Helga's night off?'

'Nice sweater, Julian,' commented Malcolm. Julian vied with Mandy in the pyrotechnics of his dress. His jersey was sky-blue with an arching salmon knitted in from shoulder to waist.

Julian was delighted to tell them about it, coming out from behind the desk to show it better. He pirouetted on white calf shoes. 'It is pretty, isn't it? I saw it in a shop window just off the Via Veneto in May and what could I do ? It was crying out to me! Who else in the wide, wide world could it have been meant for?'

'Pretty rough-looking salmon. It looks like a kelt to me,' remarked Kelvin, examining it critically.

'You want sea-lice on a sweater?' asked Julian scornfully. 'If you go to the bar, I'll come through and serve you in a couple of minutes. I'm just making out a bill.' He went back behind the desk and Malcolm led the way through to the bar. It was empty save for one ancient guest in plus-fours who was snoring in a chair by the window with a copy of *The Field* open on his lap. The rest of the hotel's occupants would be slumbering in their beds, recovering from their day's exertions on the river and preparing for the steak and kidney pudding on the evening's menu.

'It really is a pretty dire place to come for a drink,' commented the commander, glancing at the prints by Lionel Edwards and Cecil Aldin on the wall.

Malcolm looked out over the lawn in front of the hotel which stretched down to the river. 'Well, it doesn't really matter since you're not here for a drink. We might be, but you're here for information and instruction.'

'I must say, I'm finding this extremely embarrassing.'

'It's your own fault. You must be the only sailor on the seven seas who needs to be told how to act the gay.'

'Bloody homos,' muttered Kelvin. 'You know what I did today? I castrated twenty lambs with my teeth – and they're not my own teeth either. I'd like to see one of those bloody homos do something like that.'

Malcolm's face creased with pain. 'Oh dear, Kelvin, you can be positively rococo, sometimes.'

208

Julian came striding gaily into the room. 'Rococo? What do you mean, Malcolm?'

'Kelvin's talking about biting the balls off sheep.'

Julian stopped in his tracks and groaned. 'You know, I sometimes feel I should sell up and buy a garret in San Francisco. You peasants can be so earthy that you're positively subterranean.'

'It's just Kelvin,' reassured Malcolm.

'It isn't, you know,' replied Julian with a sad shake of his head. 'Anyway,' he continued, lifting the flap to get behind the bar, 'now you're here, what would you like to drink?' Julian's resident clientele liked its liquor hard and usually brown. His only draught beer was drawn straight from the barrel and tasted like ferret widdle. It won frequent awards at Real Ale festivals. Malcolm was the only member of the community who could stomach it.

'Whisky.'

'Whisky.'

'I think I'll have a pint of your best.'

Julian selected a glass and trickled a sullen pint from a dusty barrel, plonking it guiltily on the counter in front of Malcolm. The contents looked like one of those table lamps of the sixties with globules of unidentified matter swirling around in amniotic fluid. He and the other two watched, their lips curling with disgust, as Malcolm picked up his beer, took several swallows and banged it back on the bar. 'Your ale is a credit to you, Julian.'

'So it has been said.'

'By whom?' challenged Kelvin.

'Well . . . er . . . by Malcolm here for one. And . . . and . . .' Julian smacked the side of his head, 'the last customer who had some. I've forgotten who it was.'

'It was probably Malcolm the last time he was in here,' sneered Kelvin.

'Of course!' exclaimed Julian. 'You're absolutely right! It was Malcolm. I don't suppose we can really count him twice.'

Malcolm looked dubiously down at his beer. 'I haven't been in here for several weeks.'

'Well, there's not very much call for it, you see. But it's awfully nice to know you like it so much.'

The commander cleared his throat. 'Actually, we're here for a purpose – I'm here for a purpose, anyway.' He paused. 'It's difficult to know quite how to put it.'

'For heaven's sake, do try, dear boy. I can't stand the suspense. That's £2.30 for the drinks.'

'Well, you may have heard that I've got problems with Mandy.'

Julian gave a little shiver. He could have been a character in a sitcom produced by a provincial commercial television station had it not been for the shrewd, sardonic eyes through which he viewed the world and his more comely apprentice chefs. 'Yes, it must be quite thrilling for you! She seems so outrageously butch.'

'Perhaps,' agreed the commander cautiously. 'I've been trying to put her off without success for weeks and Malcolm came up with this idea that if I made out I was gay, then she'd leave me alone and we . . . er . . . thought that you might . . . you know . . .' The commander's voice trailed into embarrassed silence in the face of Julian's incredulous expression.

'What a ridiculous palaver! Why on earth don't you just tell her to piss off?'

The commander's hand shook so violently that he spilled a few drops of whisky. Since he had already wet his lips with it and it had only been a standard pub measure in the first place, he was understandably concerned. 'Bugger!' he exclaimed, carefully licking his hand. 'Look, if anybody else tells me to tell her to piss off, I shall carry out violence on sensitive portions of his anatomy.'

'Oh dear!' said Julian. 'We are touchy, aren't we? Sorry I spoke.'

'It's all right. It's just that nobody seems to be taking the situation seriously.'

'Perhaps because it's not too serious a situation,' suggested Julian.

'It's bloody serious. It's interfering with my life.' The commander had a tendency to become maudlin. He might well have dropped the odd tear into his whisky if he had not been afraid of over-diluting the tiny quantity that was left.

Julian raised his hand to scratch the back of his head. He sighed. 'All right, I accept that. But honestly, Commander, don't you think it's going a little far to proposition me? I'm awfully sorry, but I can't really say that I fancy you.' There was a snort from the chair by the window. The ancient guest was demonstrating that his hearing was still in good working order. His eyes remained closed, making it the mildest of protests.

The commander was working himself into a bit of a lather. 'No, no, no. Good God, no! What a revolting idea! I never suggested anything of the sort!'

'Commander!' exclaimed Julian, his eyes those of a down-trodden inmate of Battersea Dogs' Home, although the effect was spoiled with a wink at Kelvin. 'What a thing to say!'

'I don't mean it personally,' babbled the commander. 'If I was like that, I'm sure I'd love to.'

'Then if you want to be like that, we have no problem, have we?' Julian gave the commander a winning smile. 'Oh! This is going to be so exciting!' Julian pouted and wriggled his shoulders in a way that made the commander blench. His hand automatically lifted his glass, only to find that its contents had evaporated. Julian was right there, pouring another drink straight from the bottle: 'Have this on me.' Kelvin stirred on his stool and shifted his glass along the polished wood of the counter towards Julian. It was ignored as the commander gulped down his drink and then took a deep breath to calm himself.

'Let's start again. I'm sorry if I haven't made myself clear.'

'Oh, but you have.'

'No, Julian, I haven't. I really truly haven't. The important bit was "pretend". I want to pretend to be a poofter so that I can put Mandy off. I only want some tips on how I should do it.'

'You don't like me!' exclaimed Julian.

'No, no, no. I do like you. I really do. But,' he added

211

hastily, as Julian met his worried gaze with eyes that shone like fairy lights, 'not in that sort of way.'

'How about giving me a drink?' interrupted Kelvin.

Julian turned. 'Look, Kelvin. The day after you give me something for nothing, I shall give you a free drink.'

'That's not fair! You've poured the commander a whisky which is at least a triple!'

'A triple? Was it a triple?'

'Yes, it damn well was! In fact, it was nearer a quadruple!'

Julian went to the cash register. 'Four whiskies. That's £3.20. It is your round, isn't it, Kelvin?'

Kelvin hesitated. 'Yes! No! That's not the point. The commander didn't order it. It was free!'

'It most certainly was not! And whether he ordered it or not, he's drunk most of it. That's £3.20.'

'In that case, it's Malcolm's round.'

'I'll chalk it up on your account, Malcolm,' said Julian.

'What are you talking about? He hasn't got an account. You won't let anyone have an account here.'

'I've just opened one for Malcolm,' replied Julian blandly. 'But there's no need for him to rush to pay.' He turned his head from Kelvin, who was spluttering indignantly at being out-manoeuvred, back towards the commander. 'Look, Commander, I was just pulling your leg. I would no more fancy you than you would Mrs Baggins. I think your idea is ridiculous, but if you must do it, just flap your wrists and behave like any of the TV queers.'

The commander showed relief. 'Oh! You mean you didn't really think I wanted to . . . er . . .' He laughed heartily, but a shadow flew across his face. 'You're not saying that I'm no more attractive than Mrs Baggins, are you? I mean, you might say that about Kelvin here, but not me.'

'Oh dear!' sighed Julian, turning to Malcolm. 'These two are like Tweedledum and Tweedledee. Can't you take them away with you?'

'I'm sorry,' Malcolm apologized. 'I know what it can be like if you don't see them every day. But the commander would really appreciate any help that you might be able to give. He's really most insecure about the whole business.'

'That's right,' confirmed the commander. He hung his head, more to check whether Kelvin was trying to sneak some of his whisky than to demonstrate insecurity. 'I know it's a bit of a cheek, but you're the horse's mouth, as it were.'

Julian sniffed, looking at the commander with calculation before coming to a brisk decision. 'Right, my jolly matelot friend. I believe there's going to be Marcia's charity lunch up at the manor next week.'

'Yes,' said the commander warily. 'It's in aid of the World Wildlife Fund.'

'Just you make sure you turn up. And you can buy me a packet of David Shepherd Christmas cards so that Marcia will let me out the door afterwards.'

'Why? What are you going to do?'

'What you asked. I'm going to persuade Mandy that you're as gay as Tinkerbell.'

'Can't you just give me tips?' pleaded the commander.

'When I do a job, I do it properly.'

'But you won't create some sort of dreadful scene, will you? It's an embarrassingly public place.'

'Ah! You don't want to come out of the closet. Is that it?'

'Yes,' blurted the commander, nodding vigorously. 'That's just how I want it.'

'But the closet door to be just a teensy-weensy bit ajar so that Mandy can peek through?'

'Yes, I suppose we must allow that, but we don't want her to see anything too upsetting when she peeks, eh?'

'We'll see what we can do.' The quality of Julian's smile did little to reassure the commander.

Chapter Fourteen

MARCIA'S LUNCH happened every year and she invited everyone who did not give her the impression of being liable to pinch the silver. This had included Kelvin, but the previous year he had turned up late in a state of intoxication and, although he did not pinch a spoon, he had pinched her bottom with the ruthlessness of a lobster, so he was still *persona non grata* at the manor.

The lunch was a decorous affair. Gentry from up to thirty miles distance donned their Viyella shirts, hairy ties and pearl necklaces to mingle easily with the locals for some of whom it was the equivalent of a royal garden party. The horsehair sofas, and the worm-ridden tables which flanked them, were pushed against the walls of the drawing room while trestle tables, borrowed from the church hall, were covered in sheets and food of that peculiar variety that is never met except upon such occasions – pieces of cheddar married to pineapple chunks atop crispy biscuits, celery choking beneath cottage cheese with the texture of wet Polyfilla, miniature sausage rolls with a few grains of meat swaddled in layers of soggy pastry. The goodies – teatowels, playing cards and the like – lay in ambush on either side of the front door, womanned by Mrs Baggins and by Barbara, the widow of a colonial judge who had been forcibly retired after sentencing an African to be flogged and hanged for poaching.

The turn-out at the party was the best for years. Discussion of the impending denouement of the relationship between the commander and Mandy had been so widespread that even the budgerigar which sat suspended in its cage in the window of

214

the cafe was in on it, causing the commander to blush by screeching 'Who's a pretty boy?' whenever he walked past. Nobody wished to miss the fun.

By 1pm there was an air of expectancy in the manor. Nobody was buying and nobody was eating, although there had been a run on the wine. The furthermost flung of the visiting country gents of both sexes milled in an uneasy group near the window, sensitive to the febrile atmosphere but unaware of its cause. Mandy had the commander by a glass case containing a stuffed tapir, oblivious to the twelve-foot *cordon sanitaire* which the party had tacitly thrown round them. She was ogling him over the rim of her glass while the commander had his eyes nervously riveted on the door.

Julian arrived at 1.15. His entrance had the impact of that of Pizarro at the court of Atahualpa. Conversation amongst the locals faded into silence, isolating the voice of the middle-aged daughter of an earl who was regaling her peers by the window: '—the fucking animal refused a perfectly ordinary little hedge. It was so humiliating as Bunty knew it had cost me an arm and a leg. Damned creature was used to the pistes up in Leicestershire. I say! Why has everyone gone quiet? And who's that ghastly little poof? Is he frightfully famous or something?'

Julian stood framed in the doorway. He had dressed for the occasion with some skill, wearing a brown three-piece tweed suit, although the effect was marred by the yellow waistcoat and a large badge which stated 'I am AIDS free.' The other guests parted like the Red Sea, leaving him two clear paths radiating from the doorway – one towards Mandy and the commander and the other towards the window in case he felt like an altercation with milady whose last two sentences had fallen into the silence like an anvil into a millpond. Julian looked down the left-hand tunnel towards the commander and Mandy. She had turned and seemed puzzled. As the only person within paper-streamer range of the commander who did not know what fate had in store for them, she had every right to wonder why her companion was looking at Julian as a rabbit would a stoat and why the others round about had the air of a Roman crowd when the lion spotted a succulent Christian across a packed arena. Julian smiled a wintry smile and plunged into the crowd towards the table where the squire was dispensing drinks.

'He must be going to wait for a little while,' said Ivor.

'But why?' asked Gerald Mowbray, glancing at his watch. 'I don't want to stand around here all afternoon. I've got an artic loaded with straw coming this afternoon.'

'You don't have to stay,' said Lindy tartly.

'Nor do you, missy. You're supposed to be coming out to look at old George's leg at two. If Julian don't get on with it, you'll be late.'

'My appointments are my business.' Lindy refused to gossip, otherwise she was quite normal.

'They're mine too when I have to give the old bugger an hour off to wait for you.'

Similar scratchy conversations were taking place all over the room. The audience had expected swift action. 'What's going on, Julian?' asked the squire, as he proffered a glass of red wine. 'I haven't missed it, have I?'

Julian sipped the wine and grimaced as it slunk over his palate. 'I thought I might like a drink first, but I was wrong.'

The squire raised his voice. 'It's all right! He's going to do it in a minute!' he called.

'Do what?' came a plaintive cry from the window. 'This is a most peculiar sort of party. I can't think what Marcia's playing at.'

'Julian!' ordered the squire. 'Go and tell Lady Daphne what's going on. It's a bit unfair to leave her in suspense.'

'I'll go,' said Keith, who was standing within earshot. He wriggled swiftly through the crowd with the adroitness of the one in 300 million that succeeds in fertilizing the ovum.

Dennis took the opportunity to pass Julian a glass of whisky as the squire looked after Keith thoughtfully. 'That might be quite a good idea,' he said. 'Daphne has always prized enthusiasm above all other virtues in her lovers and one hears that Keith may be just the ticket for her.' He shook his head gloomily.

216

'Nice enough fellow, Keith. But a chap had to have something before the women would let him into their knickers in the old days.'

'It's the modern decline in morality,' agreed Julian drily.

The squire cocked an eye at his badge. 'You're right, but I don't mind buggers. Had plenty of them in the regiment and most of them were quite charming.'

'Thank you,' said Julian even more drily.

'Don't mention it. Would you like some more wine?'

'No, thank you.'

The squire grunted in disappointment. 'You'd be doing me a favour. Marcia will have me drinking the stuff for weeks.'

'Speaking of which, our hostess approaches.'

'Julian! Have I caught you in time?' Marcia was looking flushed.

'What do you mean?'

'Don't be silly! Have you done the dirty deed for the commander yet?'

'No.'

'Oh good.' She turned to her husband. 'Nobody's buying a damn thing. They're all waiting for Julian and then they'll be out the front door like lemmings.'

The squire looked round the room. 'You may well be right, dear. But I don't know what I can do about it.'

'Give them a little speech. Thank them all for coming and that sort of thing and then tell them that Julian won't be doing his thing until they've all bought something.'

The squire was aghast. 'How can I say that? They'd probably lynch me, anyway.' The mood of the party was beginning to change. Julian had played it shrewdly, but he was in danger of allowing anticipation to turn into frustration.

'I'll say something, Marcia. After all, it is me that they have come to see.'

'Yes. I've something to say about that. It's all very well to pack the house, but they're supposed to be here because they want to preserve wildlife.'

'Think like a Jesuit, Marcia. The ends justify the means.'

'But the means are the ends. If we don't get the means, the

217

Chinese mountainsides will be carpeted with dead pandas.'

'Oh dear!' remarked Julian mildly. 'There seem to be many responsibilities descending on my shoulders all of a sudden. I have a sudden urge to discharge them. Excuse me.' He put a hand on the table and climbed up on a chair. He clapped his hands for silence as Marcia looked worriedly at the chair. The furniture of the manor had been an important breeding habitat for woodworm for centuries. The conversation died to a buzz and then into silence.

'Ladies and Gentlemen, I'm sure we all know why we're here by now.' There was a murmur of excitement. He was going to make a speech.

'He's going to announce that the commander is a poof!' exclaimed Ivor. 'That's subtle!'

There was a sudden cry from the opposite corner. 'Julian! *No!*'

'It's all right, Commander.' Julian raised a propitiatory hand. 'I would like to thank everyone for coming and our particular thanks go to the squire for lending his lovely home once again and to Marcia for providing this delicious lunch. However, I can assure you that it was not my hotel that did the catering.' There was a polite laugh: a little barbed but adequately witty seemed to be the consensus. 'Marcia informs me that unless you all go and spend your money in the hall, our planet will be smothered in decomposing pandas. I shall wait patiently here as you do so. I won't do anything until you're all back.' There was a delay of several seconds while the audience assessed Julian as he stood with folded arms on the chair, a slight smile playing about his lips. Then it broke in a great surge towards the doors. Julian watched them stream through into the hall. 'I'd get back to your post, Marcia.'

'Yes, I will. Thank you very much. I'll wink at you or something when the time is right.' She turned to plunge into the sea of people.

'What a peculiar speech!' said Mandy. 'And why was Julian making it?'

'I can't imagine,' the commander replied.

'Are you all right? You look a little flushed.'

'It's just the heat,' said the commander, fishing a handkerchief from his pocket and wiping beads of nervous sweat from his forehead.

It was fifteen minutes before the roar of the market place died down and people trickled back into the sitting room clutching their knick-knacks. Julian had stayed by the drinks table to demonstrate that he was keeping his side of the bargain until Marcia waved her arm at him above the crowd. Once again the sea parted, revealing a stained brown carpet, now decorated with discarded gherkins and the odd dollop of cottage cheese, stretching towards the small pool of conversation to which Mandy and the commander were contributing. The commander watched him approach, an expression of resolution on his face. This moment was the culmination of months of hope and a week of nail-biting anticipation. He knew that what was to follow would be a grim, unpleasant business but, as a trained warrior, he realized that one sometimes had to endure the agony and humiliation of battle in order to achieve a lasting peace. He had done his best to ensure that everyone knew he was not really gay, whatever happened.

Julian processed along the ranks with his hands behind his back, nodding and smiling at friends and pausing every few yards to drop a sentence or two of greeting to a privileged guest. The squire, appropriately, walked a few deferential paces behind in attendance.

Julian emerged into the clearing surrounding the commander's group. The commander took a deep breath and cleared his throat. 'Harrumph! Er . . . hello, dear.'

Mandy swivelled to see who the commander was addressing and hit a smear of lumpfish roe. Julian stepped nimbly backwards as she flailed her arms before crashing forward on her hands and knees. Keith knew there was trouble brewing. Left to herself – and those surrounding were showing little interest in helping her to regain her poise and her feet – she would incandesce her surroundings in a holocaust of invective

219

which would render the execution of their carefully constructed plan impossible. Mandy's outbursts of vituperation could only be enjoyed out of doors, otherwise the spectator risked immolation. He shimmied through the crowd, doing his spermatozoa impression, to her side and wrapped her in solicitude.

'Mandy!' he cried, as he hauled her to her feet. 'Are you all right? Oh dear! You must have fallen right on a cream cheese and anchovy canapé!' He dabbed at the stain with his finger. 'No! It's the garlic dip! We'll have to get a new dress.' Mandy stood, looking about her like a bull facing the banderillero. The Lady Daphne, who had followed Keith through the crowd dragging a young man of good but vacant looks in her wake, was unwise enough to laugh. It gave Mandy her target. 'Shut up, slag!' she snarled.

'Well really!' The Lady Daphne did not know the danger that she was courting, but others did. The squire retreated hurriedly from the area of peril, using as an excuse the need to gather up the contents of Mandy's handbag which had burst open upon impact with the floor, scattering lipsticks, half-litre bottles of scent and deodorants, powder and paint over a good part of the room. 'How dare you speak to me like that, you ridiculous person!'

'Ridiculous! You call me ridiculous!'

'Darling!' interrupted Keith feebly.

'Keep out of this, you useless turd!' snapped Mandy.

The commander was standing behind the infuriated Mandy, hoping that out of sight meant out of mind. His proximity to the emotional napalm that was roaring out of her had driven the Grand Plan from his mind and he was concentrating on nothing more than his own survival.

Julian, however, was cast in the mould of Cromwell, Churchill or Paisley. He knew a crisis when he saw one and dealing with them was part of his trade. He assessed the situation with a calculating eye, seeking both the best way to distract Mandy before she tore the throats out of those in her vicinity and still achieve the purpose of the afternoon. 'Commander! Are you all right?'

The commander let out a small squeak of fear at having attention drawn to him. 'Eh? What? Yes, of course I'm all right. Why shouldn't I be?'

Julian laid a hand on the commander's arm. 'Oh! Thank God! I couldn't have coped if you had been hurt.' He moved forward and, in full view of the company and less than six feet away from Mandy, he kissed the commander lightly on the cheek. It happened too quickly for the commander to take evasive action; his hand flew to his face and his guilty eyes first to Julian and then to Mandy. Julian was looking quietly pleased with himself. Mandy was not, but at least her mind had been taken off her immediate troubles.

'You're queer,' she stated flatly. 'You're nothing but a nasty little queer. I might have bloody well known it.'

'Not a nasty little queer,' protested Julian. 'He's nice and really rather attractive.'

'You keep quiet,' said Mandy without taking her eyes off the commander. Nor did at least another fifty speculating pairs round about. 'Why didn't you tell me you were queer?'

'You shit, Julian!' whispered the commander. 'I said let Mandy peek. Not rip the cupboard door off its hinges in front of half the world.'

Julian looked at the commander and shrugged. 'Under the circumstances I had to do something rather drastic. I've done

221

what you wanted. It's up to you now.'

'Commander!' roared Mandy. 'Answer my question. Why didn't you tell me?'

The commander looked at her, looked at the crowd round about which was looking back at him with hungry interest. He turned to Julian with mute appeal in his eyes.

'You were embarrassed to bring it up,' prompted the latter encouragingly.

'I was embarrassed to bring it up,' parroted the commander. He grimaced as he finished his sentence and fired a dirty look at Julian who shrugged. It did sound a bit feeble. Mandy certainly thought so.

'You bloody little wimp! You fooled us all! Even my blasted husband said you fancied me!' The mob sighed its pleasure.

'Well, I did – I mean I do, of course. I'm not that queer.'

'He'd have to be bloody queer to fancy her,' remarked the Lady Daphne to general murmurs of agreement, once it was clear that Mandy had not heard her.

'You bastard! I've been wasting my time over you for months and you're not even attractive! I'll kill Keith. Where is he?' She looked round, but her husband had melted into the crowd.

The commander frowned once more. 'You mean you don't fancy me?'

'Christ, no,' answered Mandy, witheringly. 'Your moustache is even worse than Keith's. But if you're my age and married to someone like him, you don't look a gift horse in the mouth.'

'I always check a gift horse myself, in case it might be pregnant with ill-disposed Greeks,' contributed Julian.

'You shut up!'

'Sorry.'

Mandy glared at the commander. 'At least most queers are honest these days. I hate the sneaky ones like you. I'm cancelling my sprouts order, you fairy.'

'Mandy! I'm not gay!'

But she tossed her chin contemptuously and walked through the crowd to the door.

'Well, it worked,' said Julian as conversation started up behind her.

'But it was all unnecessary,' moaned the commander. 'She thinks I'm gay. And she says I'm unattractive. It's awful.'

'It doesn't really matter. There are worse things that can be thought about you.'

'I need a drink,' said the commander. 'This is a nightmare! Half these people don't know I'm not gay. What can they be thinking?' He turned and bumped into Lady Daphne's escort. 'What do you want?' he demanded.

'I was just coming to say that you handled a difficult situation extremely well.'

The commander looked for irony but found none. 'Thank you.'

'I thought you might like a decent drink.' He pulled a glass flask covered in crocodile skin from the inner pocket of his tweed suit. 'It's from a little distillery on my uncle's estate. It's just the ticket when one's shooting.'

'Aha!' cried the commander. 'Life looks up a bit. You're a man after my own heart!'

'Oh! I do hope so. I find you rather beautiful in a rugged sort of way.'

The commander turned to Julian, stifling a sob. 'What have you done to me?' he whispered.

'Don't be depressed. He finds you attractive!'

'Yes! That's true. I'm not like Mrs Baggins, am I?' He turned back to Lady Daphne's escort. 'Thank you, but go to hell and take your whisky with you.'

'But I thought—'

'You thought wrong. Talk to Julian about it. I'm going to the pub. Come on, Ivor.'

The pub was still open when the commander and Ivor arrived. Bill was by the bar along with Jimmy and both were staring ahead of them at the wall in silence. By the fire was Mandy, batting her eyelids at Kelvin who was clutching his whisky like a talisman. She had seen the commander enter but ignored him. The commander looked at her with a happy sigh. 'Perhaps it was worth it. I'll buy you a beer, Ivor. It's like coming home.'

Bill turned. 'Hullo, Commander.' He jerked his thumb towards the fire. 'It must have worked all right. She bought him a free drink as soon as she came in. Have you heard about the Mattocks?'

'No.'

'Shocking it is. Hilda Mattock poured sugar into the petrol tank of that Mary's little red car.'

'Mary?' queried the commander delicately.

'Frank's relief milker. Her with the big bosoms and a backside like a Large White sow.'

'You know what's so nice about living here?' said the commander.

Bill frowned. 'What?'

'It's the right things that are important.'

Bill shifted in his seat uncomfortably. 'I don't know about that sort of thing.'

Mandy's tinkling laugh broke the silence. The commander stiffened, but relaxed again. He sighed happily a second time. 'It'll soon be Christmas. Can I buy everyone a drink?'